The Natural Actor
Preparing for and Beginning the Journey

By Mary Kate Caffrey

cognella™
San Diego, CA

Bassim Hamadeh, Publisher
Christopher Foster, Vice President
Michael Simpson, Vice President of Acquisitions
Jessica Knott, Managing Editor
Stephen Milano, Creative Director
Kevin Fahey, Cognella Marketing Program Manager
John Remington, Acquisitions Editor
Jamie Giganti, Project Editor
Brian Fahey, Licensing Associate

First published in the United States of America in 2012 by University Readers, Inc.

Trademark Notice: Product or corporate names may be trademarks or registered trademarks, and are used only for identification and explanation without intent to infringe.

16 15 14 13 12   1 2 3 4 5

Printed in the United States of America

ISBN: 978-1-60927-270-8

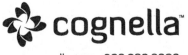

www.cognella.com 800.200.3908

Dedication

This book is dedicated to Sara E. O'Neil–Maslin

"You gain strength, courage, and confidence by every experience
in which you really stop to look fear in the face."
—Eleanor Roosevelt

Contents

Part I: Preparing the Spirit

Part 2: Beginning to Act

Part 3: Acting with Text

List of Exercises

Acknowledgments

I began this book working with brilliant educators and fellows involved in the Calderwood Teachers as Writers Fellowship at the Boston Atheneum. I cannot thank Judy Goleman and my colleagues in that program enough for their help and guidance at the beginning of my journey. Without the generosity and patience of my spouse—Brigid O'Connor—and son—Eamon Caffrey—this book would never have made it to print. I must also thank the teachers and students with whom I have discovered the joys and challenges of acting throughout the years. I am indebted to the actors with whom I have had the pleasure of collaborating. Thanks also to my parents—Dr. Robert Caffrey and Mary Lou M. Caffrey—and my brothers and sisters—Bob, Tom, Beth and Peggy—for their love and support. Special thanks go to: Nan Withers-Wilson; Dawn Mora; Richard Toma; Robert Chapline; and David Mold. Thanks also to Dave Nuscher for early editing and feedback on the text. So many things in life take a village, unfortunately I don't have room to thank all of the villagers who helped me to make this book happen. I can only hope that you know who you are.

Introduction

Philosophy of the Approach

This book's approach to the art of acting deals first with addressing the actor's instrument—body, voice, imagination, creativity, and spirit. Through skill-developing exercises, play, and journal work, the student is encouraged to break down the "blocks" to creativity and expressiveness that she has developed throughout her life. The technique employed in this book challenges each student to consider the work from a place of abundance. The student is reminded throughout that she had the skills and freedom she needed to be an actor when she was a child. Most children enjoy a body, voice, and imagination that are fully engaged. Children have an innate desire to "play" and believe in what they are playing. This skill can be reawakened through understanding the theory and practicing the work in this book. All you need to bring with you is determination, an open heart and mind, and—as one of my students once said—"the faith of a child."

Process, Not Product

"Patience, Grasshopper"

Training to be an actor is a long process. This process may be fun. It may be exciting. It may be liberating and freeing. However, as you embark on this process, you must accept that it takes time. You have the ability. You were born with it. Now you must summon the courage, trust, and determination to discover this talent anew. When you are beginning, you must have the will to focus on the process—your training. Don't worry about the product—your performance.

You have no way of knowing where this journey will take you. You don't know what lies around each bend. That is where courage comes in. You must be willing to go ahead, even when you sense that you don't know where you are going or why. This is where trust comes in. You must trust your instrument—body, voice, imagination, creativity, and spirit. Sometimes an exercise may touch on something that moves you (physically, emotionally, psychologically, or spiritually) in a way that you sense you have never been moved before. This may frighten you or shock you. You may resist. Try not to resist. Accept the process. Have patience with yourself and the process. That is where the determination comes in.

Trust your instrument. It is taking you on a journey that may lead to what are often called "breakthroughs." Breakthroughs are just that—an actor "breaks through" a block in her instrument and takes a step forward. The energy behind a "breakthrough" is palpable. The actor grows and changes. As an actor becomes increasingly skilled, she realizes that these "breakthroughs" are just a part of the process. They happen when the actor least expects them. But they do happen. It just takes time, courage, trust, patience, and determination.

The focus of Western society is primarily on product. "What grade did you get?" "What are you going to be when you grow up?" "What do you do for a living?" "How much money do you make?" "How many children do you have?" There is little patience, and even less trust—especially of the unknown. An actor must reverse this type of thinking in herself. She must learn a different focus. Training to be an actor begins with a focus on process, not product. Embrace the process. Trust that, eventually, you will be able to produce a product. Once you are working as an actor, the process of creating the part and the process of sharing that creation with an audience is your goal. Acting is a process that you share with others, both your fellow actors and an audience. The process never ends, as long as you continue to be an actor. Even when an actor is not working on a play, she is always training, changing, and growing.

As you work through this book, you may feel yourself wanting to rush ahead to the next thing. If this happens, slow down and remind yourself to "enjoy the process." That is the only way you will reap the rewards of the work. Have patience. Be courageous. Work hard. Enjoy and embrace the process.

Journaling Technique

Reflecting on and recording of process and growth are important and rewarding parts of the journey of becoming an actor. In this book, the student actor will come across questions and statements that will prompt him to record his thoughts, feelings, and discoveries as he begins to release the actor within. For the open response prompts, I suggest that the student write the prompt and then continue to let his pen move across the paper. Anything goes. He can draw words or pictures, write complete thoughts or incomplete thoughts. He can write in any language. The writing does not have to make any logical sense and he shouldn't edit himself. If he is stuck, he can write "blah, blah, blah" or just doodle until something comes into his mind. He mustn't judge what he's written or drawn. He may come back to the journal later and reflect on it if he chooses. There is no right or wrong in this type of journaling. The journal is a place to reflect and respond to the process. I also suggest that the student set a time limit for journaling and stick to it (30 seconds, 1 minute, 5 minutes). Keep the pen moving the entire time. Don't stop to think. Don't stop moving the pen until the allotted time has expired.

This type of freedom in writing may seem daunting at first. Even if it is hard, encourage yourself to persist. Being persistent in the face of difficulty is an important skill for an actor to learn. Acting is not easy; it takes patience and persistence.

Part 1
Preparing the Spirit

What Do I Need to Get Started?

The Three C's: Courage, Cooperation, and a Willingness to Change

Chapter 1

What is Acting?

What is Acting, Really?

Acting is the art of make-believe. It is pretending to be another living entity, and investing your body, mind, and spirit into playing that entity to the best of your ability. Acting is an innate human need. Anthropologists have observed the need for play-acting in all cultures. It is one of the ways that humans communicate with and learn from one another. An actor keeps her audience engaged when she "act outs" her story. In doing this, she may imitate a living being's voice, facial expression, walk, or gesture. She may attempt to alter her voice and body so that her audience can more fully experience the event she is communicating. An actor does actions that move an audience to experience an event through their mind, emotions, and body.

In communicating her event, she will leave out details—those that don't excite or interest the audience. Her story does not imitate events as they actually took place. The storyteller chooses the most exciting and compelling moments and reenacts them. Like all artists, the storyteller must delve into the chaos of the details of an event, and bring order. Through this process, she will interpret and find meaning in that event. The actor, like all artists, must be trained to create his art—to bring order to chaos.

Acting exists in all cultures. Styles of acting differ from culture to culture and from century to century. However, all acting has four common elements. These are:

Focus and Dedication

All accomplished actors train in technique. Like a dancer, athlete, martial artist, or anyone else who uses her body as her "tool" or instrument, an actor in any tradition must commit to daily mental and physical work throughout her career. Acting is a vocation that requires this type of diligent resolve.

Movement and Intensity

Acting is art. It is not real life. It is bigger than real life and yet it is also real. The actor communicates to her audience visually and orally. She creates with her total being. She connects with her audience through the intensity of her physical and vocal expression.

Imagination and a Playful Attitude

Acting requires an imagination. Most humans are born with an active imagination. An actor must constantly develop her ability to imagine. As we age, this becomes more difficult for some. An adolescent or adult may attempt to control or negate his dreams and fantasies for fear of being considered childlike—or worse. One of the requirements of acting IS being childlike when performing. A child is willing to take risks, is physically and vocally expressive, has a vivid imagination, is curious about the world, is determined to get what she wants, is vulnerable to the world around her, and is very good at reading the "moods" of the people in her environment. For children, life and learning is play. The mind of a child is incredibly inventive. If an event in a child's life is painful or difficult, she will use her imagination to change that event into something that she can tolerate. She will transfer her feelings onto a toy, drawing, or character she creates. She will then "act out" the event, using her imagination to explore and understand her feelings.

All of these whimsical qualities also engender a great actor. If an adult training as an actor has lost this inventive and lively ability, it must be developed.

Transformation

Throughout history, the ability of great actors to morph into another living being has often been perceived as something "magical." This capability has been considered by many to be inexplicable because some "brilliant actors" accomplish this feat with seemingly little effort. When an audience witnesses an exhilarating and emotionally moving performance, they will refer to an actor's "talent" or "gift." This power is an important one. It is easier for some people than others. Some people, due to their nature and life circumstances, find it easier to access this capability. However, most have the means to tap into this "gift." Those who do it well are fortunate enough to understand the importance of developing the first three elements of acting noted above: Focus and Dedication; Movement and Intensity; and Imagination and a Playful Attitude.

Discipline

Acting requires a tremendous amount of discipline. When most people hear the word "discipline," they think "punishment" or "being disciplined" by someone else. In the beginning of training, you may have an instructor giving you some structure or rules to follow. However, it is imperative that you develop self-discipline. If you are a student who has trouble with self-discipline, learning to act may help you to improve your self-discipline.

What kind of discipline does acting require? It requires many kinds. The more disciplined you are, the better actor you will become.

There are four types of discipline that an actor will develop: physical, vocal, mental/intellectual, and discipline as a team player.

Physical Discipline

An actor trains his body to respond to stimuli. The student actor will create a routine or habit of taking care of his body. He must constantly remember that his body is his instrument—the "machine" or tool that he uses to express himself on stage or screen. His "machine" must be strong, flexible, and have stamina. Like an athlete or dancer whose body is his instrument, an actor has a disciplined daily regimen. He creates this regimen for himself and executes it on his own. It is unlikely that he will have the luxury of a coach to assist him. An actor learns to treat his body like it is his most prized possession. What does the body—or any machine—need to function well?

> *Open response journal entry #1*
>
> *Write in your journal using the following prompts:*
>
> - *Discipline is ...*
> - *I can be disciplined about something ...*
> - *A time I can remember that I was very disciplined was ...*
> - *I was very disciplined at this time because ...*
> - *A time when I was self-disciplined was ...*
> - *I had a lot of self-discipline at this time because ...*

Give it good fuel—eat healthy foods and drink plenty of water. Keep the parts moving and fluid—build strength, flexibility, and stamina through daily physical exercise. Give the machine some downtime—make sure you get enough rest. Don't clog up the machine by putting things into it that will make it break down—avoid recreational drugs, smoking, and excessive use of alcohol.

Vocal Discipline

An actor possesses the discipline to free her natural voice and increase her vocal range and flexibility. She will also master as many dialects as she can. Her voice must be strong and available to express the subtle nuances of all that a character feels. If she is going to work on stage, she will communicate to audiences that vary in size from 50 to over 500 people. She may have to sustain nine performances per week. This will put a tremendous strain on her voice. If her voice is not "in shape," she may "lose" it or (even worse) do permanent damage to her vocal instrument.

Building vocal strength, flexibility, and stamina requires discipline. Vocal exercises and warm-ups, which include relaxation, alignment, breathing, resonance, and articulation, must be done frequently to keep the voice in shape. An actor trains and maintains her voice like a classically trained singer. Along with doing frequent vocal warm-ups, she must try to avoid smoking or secondhand smoke, liquor, recreational drugs, and excessive caffeine. These substances harm the voice.

Mental/Intellectual Discipline

Get out and explore the world. Read plays—one a week is a doable goal. Immerse yourself in art and culture. Keep a journal that reflects your life and the world as you experience it. Awaken your senses as much as possible. Be intellectually curious. Learn as much as you can about people throughout history from all over the world. Get used to doing research—you will be doing it for the rest of your life. Work your memorization muscles. Try to have at least 10 monologues in your stable of audition pieces at all times. Commit seven minutes a day to memorizing a monologue or some other text.

Discipline as a Team Player and Respect

In addition to coming to all classes and rehearsals with an instrument that is in good shape, an actor is a disciplined participant when working with others. Acting is a collaborative art form. People must rely on each other to create this kind of art. It is important that an actor develop respect for himself and his coworkers. Respect for self and others are very important aspects of discipline. It is a vital element of communication. Acting is all about communication. The actor communicates his wants, needs, feelings, and desires clearly to others on stage through his body and voice. Actors, directors, designers, administrators, and technicians work together to communicate a message to an audience through a production. Without respect and discipline as a team player, successful communication is not possible.

· ·

Respect Exercise

Step 1: Break up into groups of four or five. Let each person in the group tell a story about a time he was not treated with respect. Let him talk without interruption. After he has finished telling the story, ask him for any additional details you might need to better understand the situation. If he has not expressed how being disrespected made him feel, ask him to try to explain his feelings. Do not comment or judge, just gather information.

Step 2: Break up into different groups of four or five. Let each person in the group tell a story about a time that he treated someone with disrespect. Use the same guidelines as in Step 1.

Step 3: Break up into different groups of four or five. Let each person in the group tell a story about a time he was treated with respect. Use the same guidelines as in Steps 1 and 2.

· ·

Open response journal entry #5

Write in your journal using the following prompts:

- *Look up a dictionary definition of respect. After you have read it, write: Respect is ...*
- *I do/do not think respect is something that is earned because ...*
- *Self-respect is ...*
- *I do/do not think that I should treat everyone with respect because ...*
- *I do/do not think respect might affect the discipline of the group because ...*

Open response journal entry #6

Write in your journal using the following prompts:

- *Things that were evident in most of the stories about being disrespected by others are ...*
- *Things that were evident in most of the stories about being disrespectful to others are ...*
- *Things that were evident in most of the stories*

about being treated with respect are ...

- *Considering what I know from my own life and what I have heard in these stories, I think respect improves communication in the following ways ......*
- *Considering what I know from my own life and what I have heard in these stories, I think disrespect contributes to miscommunication in the following ways ...*
- *I think respect and discipline as a team player are/are not linked because ...*

Developing discipline takes practice. Treating others with respect also takes practice. If you are not taught to respect others as a child, you need to learn to practice it as an adult. Some simple ways to develop discipline and respect for the group are:

- Practice showing up on time (or better yet, early!) for all scheduled rehearsals and/or classes.
- Practice being prepared by doing your homework (i.e., memorizing your lines, working on objectives and physical actions, learning dialects, researching character choices, etc.)
- Practice accepting well-meant and constructive criticism from people who have more experience and knowledge than you do.
- Practice always trying your hardest and never giving up working on things that are within your control.
- Practice letting go of those things that are not within your control.
- Practice accepting that we are all flawed human beings who make mistakes.

Focus and Concentration

The easiest way for me to explain the importance of focus and concentration is to tell a story.

I sit in the hallway of an old school (without open windows or air conditioning) on a scorching hot July afternoon waiting for my five-year-old who is taking a dance class. On the floor is a little boy, probably about six years old. He has a basket filled with the following toys: an R2D2 robot that lights up; a bobble head football player; a plastic boat; a small Darth Vader doll; a plastic monkey; and a Ninja Turtle. This boy has created a whole world with these toys and his imagination. He is making up text—the figures are talking to each other. Each figure has his own voice and movements. The young boy creates music in the background for the "physical" moments that don't have words. He uses lots of space. He is in his own world. He is interested. He is engaged. He is completely absorbed in what he is doing. There is a tremendous amount of noise and distraction in his environment that could easily break his attentiveness. There is classical music coming from the ballet class. There is hip hop music coming from the modern jazz class. Two moms are having a conversation. The boy's baby brother is crying. A toddler is trying to take the boy's toys away from him. It is extremely hot. There is an old, very loud fan blowing warm air. There are many hindrances, and yet this young boy's center of attention is strong and complete. His "playing" is the most important thing in the world to him at this moment. When the focus and concentration is broken, his "play" will be over; the world he has created will exist no more. He will be taken out of "the moment." As long as his "play" is interesting and fun to him, his attentiveness will persist.

We can learn many things about performance from this little boy playing and creating his own "production" with words, movement, music, relationships, and spectacle. However, what I find most impressive is his focus and concentration.

People are born with varying abilities to focus and concentrate. For many, the ability to be absorbed in play dwindles with age. The mind becomes full of the "stuff" that makes up life. Some adults still have the ability to hold a center of attention with great intensity. They can get "lost" in a book or a TV show. However, if you add noise, heat, and other distractions, concentration and focus are often broken.

There are noises and distractions all over a theater during a performance: technical and mechanical noises, audience members make noise, lights go on and off, sound effects happen, etc. A movie set is even worse: microphones hang all around, camera and sound people move equipment around, planes may fly overhead, etc. Actors, like the young boy in the story, must be able to focus and concentrate even when there are many distractions. How does an actor learn to do this? In fact, an actor needs to relearn this skill. A child has the ability to remain fully engrossed during play whenever he uses his imagination. As long as his imagination is engaged, a child will continue to keep the play alive. If a child is allowed to play, without judgment, he can lose himself in the fun and excitement of creating and doing. This is one way that a child learns, by trying things out safely through play.

One other gift a child has is the ability to see the world in detail. If you allow a child to walk at her own pace, it takes a long time to get anywhere. With each step, she makes a new discovery in her world. She will focus, concentrate, and discover the world through all of her senses. Children are enthralled with the world around them. It is new. It is exciting. As children grow and repeat experiences over and over, these experiences tend to become less and less interesting. Life begins to take on a "sameness" day in and day out. Most adults do not view each day as a new experience. As a child grows into adulthood, he stops noticing the small details of life: the colors, the textures, the sounds, the smells, and the tastes. He may move into his head and away from his senses. Big events that are experienced may awaken his senses, focus, and concentration; but day–to–day life becomes less interesting. An actor must reawaken his childlike ability to experience the world around him. An actor must allow himself to slow down and see, hear, feel, smell, and taste his life as he lives it. He needs to reconnect with a child's gift of unwavering engagement through imagination and the senses.

Open response journal entry #7

Write in your journal using the following prompts:

- *I think this little boy could focus and concentrate so well, despite many distractions, because ...*
- *The last time I can remember being totally absorbed by something, I was ...*
- *The thing that broke my attention was ...*
- *When my focus and attention were broken, I felt ...*
- *I find it hard to focus and concentrate when ...*
- *I find it easy to focus and concentrate when ...*

Focus and Concentration Sensory Exercise

Step 1: Touch. Break up into pairs. Have one member of each pair blindfold the other. The student who is not blindfolded (N) hands the blindfolded student (B) an object that she has not seen. B describes what she feels to N, and N records it. B has 30 seconds to describe the object through her sense of touch. She should be specific.

Step 2: Sound. B has 30 seconds to make sound with the object and describe the sounds that the object makes. N records what she says.

Step 3: Smell. B has 30 seconds to smell the object and describe what it smells like. N records what she says.

Step 4: Taste. B has 30 seconds to taste the object and describe what it tastes like. N records what she says.

Step 5: Switch observers and recorders. The object is put away and the blindfold is removed and placed on N, who is given a different object which he must describe in 30 seconds through his senses of touch, sound, taste, and smell. B records the descriptions. The object is removed and the blindfold is put away.

Step 6: Sight. Students break up into different pairs and sit with their backs to each other. Student D has an object that student C has not seen. Each student takes a turn describing what he sees to his partner without telling him what the object is (Example: My object is small, round, black, heavy, has arms, etc.) The students who is not speaking records what her partner says.

Step 7: Reveal. Objects are revealed to the entire class. The entire class must reach a consensus and connect each object with its touch, taste, smell, and sound description from a distance.

Step 8. Consensus. The entire class should use the sight description to reach a consensus of the final determination in matching an object to its description.

Boundaries and Communication

What is a boundary? A boundary is "something that indicates a border or limit." Boundaries may be physical, social, emotional, vocal, spiritual, etc. An actor learns to set some boundaries for himself and those with whom he is working. An actor's work is intimate and personal. It requires focus, concentration, vulnerability, a playful attitude, sensitivity toward others, and an ability to accept criticism. Consider the boundaries that might help you to open up and try all of these things. Articulate what "limits and borders" you need to feel safe enough to do the work that must be done. As you get more comfortable with the work and begin to feel safe with yourself and others, these boundaries may change. If the boundary changes affect others, communicate the changes to those with whom you are working.

When you feel ready, share this information with those with whom you are training. Remember, this is only a starting point. Additional boundaries may come up as the work continues. You may not know you have a physical boundary until you are touched during an exercise. You may not know you have a vocal boundary until you are asked to yell something vulgar at your classmate. Respect your boundaries. With time you may let down some of your boundaries. As your acting skills develop, you will come across roles that require you to let go of additional personal boundaries. The choice is always yours to make. No one can make you break down a boundary. Do it in your own time as you begin to feel safe with yourself and your fellow actors. Keep the dialogue open. Don't be afraid to communicate when a boundary comes up or falls down. Communication is the key to moving forward. Indeed, open communication is one of the "keys" to acting. Once you have established some boundaries within which to work, you can move on to developing trust.

> *Open response journal entry #9*
>
> *Write in your journal using the following prompts:*
>
> - *To concentrate, I need …*
> - *I can have a playful attitude when …*
> - *It's easiest for me to be sensitive toward other when …*
> - *I can be physically intimate in class if …*
> - *Vulnerability is …*
> - *I can be vulnerable when …*
> - *Focus is …*
> - *I can focus best when …*
> - *I think criticism is …*
> - *It is easy for me to accept criticism when …*

Trust

When a baby enters the world he is totally dependent and he must "trust" that he will be taken care of. He cannot survive without other people. When a baby cries, he "trusts" that he will be fed, changed, held, entertained, quieted, etc. If his needs are met, the trust will grow. However, at some point in his life his needs will not be met, and his ability to trust others—and himself—will be affected. Perhaps it is part of a person's nature to trust?

The following trust exercise is meant to aid the actor in his journey to develop trust. For some, this exercise is easy; for others, it is very difficult. The important thing is to try and to keep on trying. Trust needs to be built. Developing a strong foundation of trust is a necessity for an actor. Keep putting down the bricks that form a foundation of trust, one at a time. Keep trying, and you will find that you soon will have built a strong foundation of trust. It's okay to be afraid. Try to work through the fear to a place of trust.

• •

Trust Exercise

Step 1: Work with a partner of approximately the same size and strength. One person (C) should stand behind the other (F), facing her partner's back. The person behind is the "catcher" (C) the person in front is the "faller" (F).

Step 2: C puts her hands up behind F, palms flat, one hand behind the shoulder blades, one hand on the lower back.

Step 3: F's feet stay parallel and a shoulder width apart.

Step 4: C is no more than a few inches away from F.

Step 5: F falls back into C's hands without turning his head or looking behind him.

Step 6: C catches F and then gently pushes him back to a standing position.

Step 7: C then takes a small step back.

Step 8: F drops back into C's hands again without looking back. F will fall a little farther this time and must trust that the he will be caught and supported by C.

Step 9: F and C repeat this sequence, with C taking small steps away from F, and F falling farther down toward the ground without turning around. F should not turn his head, stop, or brace himself.

Step 10: As C moves farther back and down, she will bend her knees and put her legs in a "thrust" position so that she doesn't hurt her back. The pair should go as far as C feels she can safely support F's fall back.

Step 11: C and F now switch roles. C will become the faller (F) and F will become the catcher (C).

Fear and Exhilaration

There is always risk involved in performance—risk of "success," risk of "failure," risk of making a fool of yourself. This element of risk creates a certain amount of anxiety and fear. Performance anxiety is a very real, physically intense experience. I have never known an actor, director, designer, or technician who wasn't at least a little anxious at a show's opening. Many directors are concerned if an actor is not nervous before he steps on stage. With fear and nerves comes an incredible amount of energy. This energy is powerful and very useful to an actor. But he must learn to harness this energy and use it to his benefit. The first step in harnessing this energy is to step into the fear and fully experience it. Don't think of fear as negative. Fear is a very healthy and useful response. As performers, we must acknowledge, accept, embrace, and move through our fear. On the other side of the fear of taking a risk is exhilaration.

When students are afraid to engage in an exercise, I often refer to taking this risk as "jumping off a cliff into the water below." This analogy is a reality for students at an unusual school in the San Francisco Bay Area. This school is run by Sam Keen, who has for many years taught everyday people with no special gymnastic ability how to perform on the flying trapeze. This is a skill that requires you to climb a

Open response journal entry #11

Now that you have tried this exercise, write in your journal using the following prompts:

- *Trust is ...*
- *If I trust people they will ...*
- *If I trust people I will ...*
- *If I don't trust people they will ...*
- *If I don't trust people I will ...*
- *I think trust is a good/ bad thing because ...*
- *If someone told me that anyone could learn to trust, I would say ...*

Write in your journal
using the following
prompts:

- When someone asks me
  to do something that is
  "risky," my first response
  is ...
- I do/do not like to take
  risks because ...
- I will take a risk if ...
- The biggest risk I've taken
  in my life is ...
- When I took this risk,
  what happened was ...
- The positive things about
  taking this risk were ...
- The things that didn't
  seem positive about
  taking this risk were ...
- When I think about
  performing in front of
  other people I physically
  feel ...
- When I imagine in my
  mind's eye what it will be
  like to perform, I see ...

skinny ladder 25 feet into the air, take a leap into space, and trust that you'll catch hold of a little piece of wood hung between two swinging ropes. Once they get to the top of the ladder, many of his students are paralyzed by fear, even though there is a net to catch them when they fall. "The object is not to conquer fear, but to become a connoisseur of fear. We teach our students to identify fear—to be aware of the physical sensations of panic and fear. What happens to them when they finally do go off the platform is that the anxiety is translated into excitement. What was terror becomes joy." It is precisely by sacrificing their safety and facing their fears that these students attain a sense of mastery, competence, and exhilaration.[1] And so it is with acting. Once you sacrifice the "safety" that keeps you in your seat and embrace the "risk" of getting up in front of an audience, your fear will become joy. Your panic and anxiety will become exhilaration that will leave you with a feeling of mastery and competence. Trust yourself and your fellow actors. Embrace your fear. It's not a chance if you don't take it. Take the chance. You will be richly rewarded if you do.

Creating a Safe Space

Learning to act is full of risks. As an actor learns her craft, there is a good deal of unpredictability, uncertainty, instability, and insecurity involved in the process. An actor must be able to "put herself on the line" and open herself up to the people and experiences around her. She will explore the myriad facets of her most private self and expose those to an audience. An actor must make herself susceptible to her partners and the experiences of the character she is playing. In physics, susceptibility is defined as "the ratio of magnetization to a magnetizing force." In other words, when she is confronted with a magnetizing force (an acting partner, a dilemma that she must act on, etc.), how much of her being, how many "particles" of her being will she allow to be released and pulled, or "magnetized," to this force. The more she is willing to release to the force, the better actor she will be.

As I write this, I realize that my use of the phrase "the force" sounds quite a bit like the quest of Luke Skywalker in the *Star Wars* movies. In order to channel this powerful "force" within himself, Luke must first learn to "let go" and trust his instincts. He cannot channel the power of the force until he allows himself to "let go" of his preconceived notions of power and strength that have come from the non-Jedi world. He goes to a space where he can learn. It is a place that does not have all the trappings of the power of the non-Jedi world. It is a place full

---

1   Hart, Joseph. "Trauma? Get over it. When to let go. How to heal." *Utne Reader*. July/August 2006, p. 45.

of natural power. At first, this place seems terrifying to both Luke and the audience, but as time goes on, and Luke's environment and teacher are revealed in their true light, his training ground becomes a safe place where he can rediscover the special talents he has possessed since birth, but has not had the resources to discover. Luke's natural training ground of swamps and snakes and bugs and an ancient little green monsterlike being becomes a safe haven for him. When Luke decides he must leave this place before his training is over, his teacher/mentor and the audience worry that he is not ready to face the outside world. Yoda voices his fear that Luke is not ready and that he is at a vulnerable place in his training because he has not yet mastered patience. Once he leaves Yoda's training ground, he will no longer be in a safe space. Yoda is afraid that his development and connection with the light side of "the force"—the openness, the goodness, the vulnerability, the ability to open his mind and heart to the goodness in others—will end. Yoda is afraid that the vulnerability that Luke has tapped into in this safe training ground will be exploited by those who have gone to the "dark side." But Luke proves him wrong: He is able to take the lessons he has learned with him and he has gained enough strength and self-respect to hang on to what Yoda has taught him and to continue to grow.

What can we take away from this? Learning and growth thrive in an environment that is safe. Learning, growth, and discovery require much risk, failure, perseverance, and vulnerability. If you and your partners in learning (teachers, classmates) can create an environment that feels safe, you will learn more quickly. In a safe environment, you are willing to take risks because you trust that if you do not succeed, the hurt will not be traumatic. Those who excel in any subject area are lucky enough to encounter or create for themselves a safe space to explore, challenge themselves and others, question, make mistakes, and grow. To excel in acting, you must have the same safe space. However, unlike some other subject areas, acting requires that you interact with other human beings. Therefore, it is important that you and those you are working with (teachers, classmates, etc.) work together to create an environment that is safe and encourages growth, risk taking, exploration, failure, perseverance, vulnerability, and tolerance.

Creating a safe space for all students in a class is a daunting task. A classroom is filled with individuals who bring with them extremely varied physical, cultural, emotional, and psychological histories. Some may be tempted to "skip" this step in the process because it seems like a waste of time and there are more important and pressing activities and training to get to. In my experience, creating a safe space is one of the best investments of time a class can make. If, beginning with the first day of class, an environment is created that encourages trust of your fellow classmates, the difficult and sensitive work that is involved in the process continues with fewer difficulties.

Begin the first class with simple introductions and a development of "ground rules" for the class. Much of this work will have been done in the section about boundaries and communication.

Open response journal entry #13

Write in your journal using the following prompts:

- *One place I feel safe is ...*
- *I think I feel safe in this place because ...*
- *A person who helps me to feel safe is ...*
- *I feel safe with this person because ...*
- *When I feel safe, the following things happen to my body ...*
- *When I feel safe, the following things happen in my mind ...*
- *One place I feel unsafe is ...*
- *I think I feel unsafe in this place because ...*
- *One person I feel unsafe with is ....*
- *I feel unsafe with this person because ...*

Creating a Supportive Ensemble

*I*n an acting ensemble (or class)—as in a sports team—the adage, "the group is only as strong as its weakest player" is absolutely true. Let's look at this saying from the perspective of an ensemble.

In acting, as in team sports, you must rely on your fellow teammates or ensemble members. A football team that doesn't work together and support and trust each other will never win the Super Bowl. It doesn't matter how great the quarterback is. If the front line doesn't support the quarterback, he will get sacked when the ball is snapped and the down will be over. There will be no movement forward, no touchdowns, and really no game. The quarterback needs the rest of the team to support him or he can't do his job.

It's the same in theater. If you are doing a scene with your partner and she has not prepared, is not willing to try, or won't connect with you, you cannot do your job. Blaming her will do no good. You still won't be able to do your job. Alternatively, you also can't expect your partner to "carry" you through a scene. You must do your part, or there will be no scene. You must be willing to prepare, work hard, and be physically, psychologically, emotionally, spiritually, intellectually, and vocally ready to do your job with your partner when you step up in front of an audience (public or classroom). Support all the members of the ensemble while you are working together. Participate in the group's commitment to supporting each other in the work. The following exercises can assist in the creation of a supportive ensemble.

NOTE: The following exercise, "Lifting and Chanting," will help to build trust along with creating a supportive ensemble. This exercise is difficult at first for some students. Encourage every member of the ensemble to participate fully. If, however, being lifted instills excessive fear or anxiety in a student, come back to it again later in the course of the work.

....

Ensemble-Building Exercises

LIFTING AND CHANTING

Step 1: One member of the class lies down on the floor.

Step 2: The remainder of the ensemble gathers around her body. The ensemble supports the prone actor's body as they lift her toward the ceiling. (Note: Stronger classmates should support the torso, and one person should be responsible for supporting the head.)

Step 3: The entire ensemble should be involved in the lifting. No one should "sit out." Make sure there is room for all to get at least one hand in to assist in the lift.

Step 4: As the ensemble lifts, they say her name, first very softly and then bringing the sound to a crescendo as they lift her toward the sky.

Step 5: The ensemble slowly and gently releases their classmate down toward the floor, saying her name and bringing the sound to a decrescendo as she is slowly lowered to the floor.

Step 6: The ensemble whispers the individual's name as hands are gently pulled from underneath her body.

COUNTING TO 20

Step 1: The group holds hands standing in a circle. Eyes are closed.

Step 2: Count from 1 to 20 in no particular order or pattern.

Step 3: If two people say a number simultaneously, start again at 1.

Step 4: Each time two or more people talk at once, the group goes back to 1 and starts again.

Step 5: The game ends when the group can count from 1 to 20 in no particular order of speaking and without anyone talking at the same time.

· ·

Open response journal entry #14

Write in your journal using the following prompts:

- *When I was lifting and chanting I felt ...*
- *When I was being lifted and my name was being chanted, I felt ...*
- *Something that was hard about this exercise for me is ...*
- *Something that I thought would be hard about this exercise that was not hard was ...*
- *Something that I thought would be easy about this exercise that was not easy was ...*

Open response journal entry #15

Write in your journal using the following prompts:

- *Some things I realized about myself while doing this exercise were ...*
- *Some things I noticed about other group members when we did this exercise were ...*
- *I thought this exercise would be easier/ harder than it was because ...*
- *I do/do not like to rely on other people to complete a task because ...*
- *Going back to 1 because people talked at the same time felt ...*
- *Going back to 1 because I was one of the people who talked with someone else felt ...*
- *When we got to 20 I felt ...*
- *I think we got to 20 because ...*

Write in your journal using the following prompts:

- When I realized I had to tell a stranger a scar story, I thought ...
- As I was telling my partner my scar story I felt ...
- When I was listening to my partner tell her scar story, I felt ...
- The hardest part about telling my scar story was ...
- I think this was hard because ...
- The hardest part of listening to my partner's scar story was ...
- I think this was hard because ...
- When my partner was telling her scar story she seemed ...
- When I was telling the class my partner's scar story, I felt ...
- When my partner was telling my scar story to the class, I felt ...

Stories of life's scars

Step 1: Students break up into pairs and tell each other a "scar story." A scar story is a very detailed story of how a person got a particular physical scar on his body. He should include as much detail as possible in telling the event. His partner is free to ask questions. If an ensemble member doesn't have a physical scar, she can talk about an embarrassing/scarring/ difficult moment in her life.

Step 2: Each student stands in front of the class with her partner and tells the class her partner's scar story. At the end, the class applauds wildly and cheers. The second member of the pair then tells her partner's scar story, followed by the audience's wild applause and cheering.

Chapter 2
Becoming Familiar with and Tuning Your Instrument

The Actor's Instrument

An artist uses his instrument to express his creative energies, impulses, and ideas. A musician may use a piano, violin, trumpet, his voice, etc. A sculptor may use stone, clay, wood, or another solid substance. A painter may use oils, water colors, acrylics, a brush, and canvas. What is the actor's instrument? What are the "things" an actor uses to express his creative energies, impulses, and ideas? The actor uses himself—his body, voice, mind, and spirit. Just like an artist in any other medium, the actor trains with that instrument and expects that it will work the way it is supposed to. Unlike artists in most other mediums, the instrument and the artist are one and the same. An actor must take care of his body in the same way any artist takes care of his instrument. An actor can only rely on an instrument that is in peak condition. If the instrument is tuned and free of debris, the artist may freely express his creative energies, ideas, and impulses.

To achieve and maintain "peak condition" of his instrument, an actor commits to a good deal of training. When an actor's instrument is in peak condition, it is responsive, expressive, relaxed, and strong. It is open to stimuli, and is poised and ready to react to that stimuli. A baby or small child has this type of instrument. His voice is strong and expressive. Before he learns words, he communicates what he wants and how he feels using his body and vocal sounds. He uses his entire being to communicate. The adults who are taking care of him are also hyperaware and struggle to understand the cues he is giving. This relationship between adult and child is very intense and very dynamic. It is filled with many expressive physical and vocal cues. As the child begins to learn sounds that have meaning (words), his expression (physical and vocal) becomes less dynamic. It is not necessary for him to use the same intense physical expression to let his needs be known. He now has words. When the child ventures outside of his home into social situations, he is told to use his "inside voice." As he grows, he will move from outside expressive play for the majority of his day to inside structured days at school. As the years progress, he will spend more and more time at a desk being quiet, and less and less time moving his body and physically expressing himself. Society will reward him for being controlled in his speech, expression, and physical movement. If he is loud, emotional, and very physical, he will be told to "calm down." He will learn that it is unacceptable to use his voice and body to its full expressive extent. When he does, he may be punished or ridiculed. This will create tensions in his voice and body and he will suppress many of the natural gifts he was born with that enable him to communicate unreservedly. He will express himself primarily with words, and limited facial expression and gesture. If he decides that he would like to pursue a career as a performing artist, he will need to reawaken his natural ability to use his entire being to express himself. This will take some time. He will need to break the habits he has fallen into as he has grown, and for which he has been commended. These are habits he has been practicing since he first started his formal education in a structured school environment.

Relaxation, Alignment, and Actor's Neutral

Excess tension in the actor's body creates "blocks" to the seamless physical and vocal expressions that give rise to a great performance. In order for the actor's body to work at peak efficiency, her muscles must be rid of excess tension. When liberated of excess tension, which inhibits fluid, natural movement and breathing, the body and voice can react to physical, emotional, and spiritual impulses quite readily.

The release of unnatural tensions in the actor's body will also lead her body to fall into proper alignment. When a body is in proper alignment, every physical action and vocal expression requires less effort. Rediscovering a relaxed and naturally aligned body takes some time and consistent effort. However, after some years of work, this state can be maintained through a daily physical and vocal warm-up.

Acting exercises often begin in what is called "actor's neutral." Actor's neutral indicates that the actor's body is in an unrestricted, restful state. This state may be achieved in a standing, sitting, or lying down (supine) position. Once an actor's body has been trained to release the tensions that hinder natural physical and vocal expression, she can attain actor's neutral instantaneously when she begins to work on a role. At the beginning of her training, however, she will want to survey her body at the outset of each task to determine that her muscles are rid of superfluous tightness that will pull her body out of alignment.

. . . .

Practicing Actor's Neutral

STANDING IN ACTOR'S NEUTRAL

Step 1: Feet are a shoulder width apart.

Step 2: Knees are slightly bent (not locked), reducing the curve in the lower back.

Step 3: The weight is evenly distributed over both feet and is felt on the whole foot (toes, balls of the feet, and heels).

Step 4: The pelvis is resting evenly over both legs.

Step 5: Feel the spine rising out of the center of the pelvis, up through the middle of the torso, all the way up to where the skull rests on top of the spine.

Step 6: Survey the torso, and ensure that the shoulders are relaxed and the shoulder blades are falling down along the back. The chest will feel open and wide.

Step 7: The head should feel as if it is floating on top of the spine in the center of the body. (Remember, the spine and skull are not locked together by bone, but are connected by muscles and soft tissue that create fluidity in the movement of the head on top of the spine.)

Step 8: Lift the head forward and up at the same time. Put the palm on the back of the neck, little finger toward the skull and thumb toward the back. The hand should not feel squished by the skull resting on it, but it should also not feel the head pulling away from it.

Step 9: Release the arms and allow them to relax by the sides, with the palms facing in toward the hips.

SITTING IN ACTOR'S NEUTRAL

Step 1: Choose a chair that has a hard surface for the buttocks and a straight back.

Step 2: While sitting, bend the knees at a 90 degree angle, so that the feet rest flat on the floor. If need be, move forward on the seat of the chair until the feet can be placed flat on the floor.

Step 3: Rest the weight on the sit bones, which are at the top of the legs and the bottom of the pelvis. Rock from side to side and feel the sit bones resting on the chair.

Step 4: Follow Steps 5–8 from "standing in actor's neutral."

Step 5: Release the arms and allow them to relax by the sides, elbows bent, with the palms resting on the thighs or knees (depending on the length of the arms).

NEUTRAL SUPINE (LYING DOWN)

Step 1: Lie on the back, with feet a shoulder width apart.

Step 2: Let the arms rest by the sides with enough space in the armpit to fit a chicken egg.

Step 3: Turn the palms up to receive the light from the ceiling.

Step 4: Feel the shoulders falling away from the ears, toward the floor, and toward the feet at the same time.

Step 5: Feel the spine aligned in the center of the body.

Step 6: Feel the head loosely floating above the spine—also in the center of the body.

Step 7: Lift the head forward and up at the same time. Put the palm on the back of the neck, little finger toward the skull and thumb toward the back. The hand should not feel squished by the skull resting on it, but it should also not feel the head pulling away from it.

Step 8: Release the arms again and allow them to relax by the sides with the palms facing up to receive the light from the ceiling.

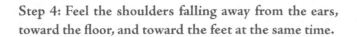

Relaxation—Becoming More Aware of The Physical Self

Many people find it difficult to truly relax their body and mind. Individuals relax in different ways. An actor must find the relaxation exercises that work best for her and practice relaxation daily. She must physically DO these exercises. She can't just think about them. There are many relaxation techniques to explore—try to find a relaxation technique that will allow you to connect your body, mind, focus, and breath. A few exercises follow.

Ground Rules

1: Make sure you find a space where you can move, stretch out, and be quiet and alone for at least 20 minutes. Get rid of anything that will distract you in the space, such as computers, TVs, telephones, people, photos, books, etc.

2: At the beginning, if you need to, put a timer on for 20 minutes. Do at least one relaxation exercise for 20 minutes three to five times per week to start.

3: Make relaxation part of your daily practice, like brushing your teeth. Set a goal—perhaps to do something to physically relax and connect with your body for at least 20 minutes every day.

• •

Relaxation "Visualization" Exercise

Do this exercise with a partner reading the description to you or record the description and listen to it as you do it.

Step 1: Lie on the floor on a towel or thin mat in "neutral."

Step 2: If you feel pain in your lower back when your legs are stretched out, bend your knees and put your feet flat on the floor until your lower back muscles begin to relax.

Step 3: Try to close your eyes. If closing your eyes makes you feel anxious or frightened, leave them open for now.

Step 4: Imagine yourself in a comfortable, safe space. Choose some place that is relaxing to you such as: a warm beach;

Open response journal entry #17

After practicing each actor's neutral position, respond in your journal to the following prompts. Create three entries: one for standing, one for sitting, and one for supine. Practice actor's neutral daily and record your responses in your journal. Notice any changes that occur.

Respond to the following prompts in as much detail as possible:

- *Right now I physically feel ...*
- *Right now I emotionally feel ...*
- *When I compare my body in actor's neutral to how it felt before I began this exercise, it feels ...*
- *As I moved into this form of actor's neutral I thought about ...*
- *During the exercise I imagined ...*
- *The parts of my body that felt awkward or uncomfortable in neutral were ...*

floating in warm water; surrounded by soft feathers; a cool moonlit night; a snow-capped mountain, etc.

Step 5: Check in with your body from head to toe. Notice where your muscles feel tight or tense. Notice where your muscles feel soft and relaxed. Notice how your clothes feel against your body. Are they tight or loose? What does the material feel like against your body? Feel the hair on your body. Feel the air against those parts of your body that are exposed. Does the air feel warm or cold? Can you feel what is happening inside your body (blood flowing, movement of the breath, saliva in your mouth, heart beating, stomach gurgling, etc.)? Are there any parts of your body that you can't feel? Don't judge, be aware.

Step 6: Bring your focus to the top of your skull. Imagine that the top of your skull is filling up with sand. Allow the muscles in your skull to become heavy and fill up with sand. Let go of tension and tightness. Feel your skull becoming heavy and giving in to the pull of gravity. Let your skull sink into the floor.

Step 7: Bring your focus down to your face. Feel the muscles in your face filling up with sand. Let the muscles in your face melt away. Let your forehead, eyes, jaw hinge, and tongue relax and soften. Let your jaw drop down to your chest. Let your breath release in and out through your open mouth and throat. Feel yourself letting go and giving in to the pull of gravity.

Step 8: Bring your focus down to your neck and throat. Feel the muscles in your neck filling up with sand. Let the muscles in your neck melt away, letting go of excess tension and tightness. Open your throat. Feel your body relax and soften. Feel your body letting go and giving in to the pull of gravity.

Step 9: Bring your focus down to your shoulders, shoulder blades in the back, and chest in the front of your body. Feel the muscles in your shoulders and upper torso filling up with sand. You may need to spend a lot of time in this area. It is not uncommon for people to be very tight in the shoulders and upper back. Let the muscles in your shoulders, shoulder blades, and chest melt away. Feel your chest opening up as your shoulders drop toward the floor. Let your muscles relax and soften. Feel your body letting go and giving in to the pull of gravity. Feel your upper torso sinking into the floor. Check in with your breath. Let it flow, nice and easy. Don't hold it. Don't try too hard, don't think about it too much. Use your imagination and try to feel your muscles melting and your shoulders letting go.

Step 10: Bring your focus down to the middle of your torso, the area around your rib cage in the front and back. Allow the muscles in your middle torso to fill up with sand and become very heavy. Let the muscles around your ribs melt away. Feel your rib cage expanding as you let the breath in and contracting as you let the breath out. Try to let go of control and let the natural rhythm of your breath take over, in and out. The more you let go and relax, the more natural and spontaneous your body will become. Feel the muscles in your mid-torso relax and soften. Feel your middle torso giving in to the pull of gravity. Feel the movement of your breath.

Step 11: Let your focus move down to your abdomen and lower back. Feel the muscles in this part of your body filling up with sand. Let the muscles in your belly and lower back melt away. Don't push your lower back into the floor. A slight curve in your lower back is natural. Let the muscles relax and soften, allowing them to be very heavy. Feel your body letting go of excess tension and tightness. Feel your spine long and wide at the same time. Let yourself lengthen and widen. Feel the space in between the vertebrae of your spine. Tell yourself to let go. Be conscious of the movement of your breath, in and out. Feel your body letting go and giving in to the pull of gravity. Allow your belly to be very heavy and wide. Try not to hold on.

Step 12: Allow your focus to move down to your pelvic area—hips, buttocks, and groin. Feel the muscles in this area of your body filling up with sand. Let the muscles in your pelvic area melt away. Let yourself relax and soften. Many people hold a lot of tension in their buttocks and groin muscles without being aware of it. Feel these muscles soft and free of excess tension. Feel your body letting go and giving in to the pull of gravity. Let your buttocks, pelvis, and groin sink into the floor. Let the tension melt away. Stay focused. Let the breath release in and out. Feel the movement of the breath in the pelvic region as you continue to let go of excess tension and tightness. Notice your physical and emotional feelings as you relax.

Step 13: Bring your focus down to your legs. Begin with your thighs. Feel the muscles in your upper thighs filling up with sand. Let them be heavy. Let the legs fall away—turning out at the hip joint, feet turned out to the side if they are not that way already. Let the muscles in your thighs melt away. Let your thigh muscles relax and soften. Feel your thighs letting go and giving in to the pull of gravity. Move the image and feeling of filling up with sand down to the knees. Let yourself be heavy and release excess tension in your knees.

Step 14: Bring your focus to the shins and calves. Let them be very soft and heavy.

Step 15: Move your focus to the ankles. Release tension in the ankles. And finally, bring the focus down to the feet. Feel the muscles in the feet become heavy and fill up with sand. Let all of the muscles in the feet—the ball of the foot, the instep, the arch of the foot, and each of the toes—give in to the pull of gravity. Let go of excess tension and tightness.

Step 16: Take a moment to feel your whole body sinking into the floor. Let your whole body give in to the pull of gravity. Let go of control. Sink into the floor. Let the tension melt away.

Step 17: Keep your mind focused on how your body feels physically. Notice those parts of your body that you can or cannot feel. Notice the natural rhythm of your breath. Notice the expansion and contraction of the body as you breathe in and out.

Step 18: Ask yourself how you feel different from the way you usually feel (physically and emotionally).

Step 19: Continue to focus on your breath, staying as relaxed as possible.

Step 20: Take a few minutes.

Step 21: If your eyes are closed, slowly flutter your eyes open.

Step 22: Without lifting your head, keeping your head and neck relaxed, roll over onto your side.

Step 23: Be aware of the rhythm of your breath.

Step 24: Curl up into a fetal position and then over onto your hands and knees.

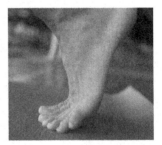

Step 25: Keep your head and neck down, curl your toes under, bend your knees, and rock back so that your feet are flat on the floor and your hips and buttocks are in the air above your head. Your arms hang loose and may come up off the floor (dropped-down position).

Spinal Roll-Up

Step 1: Slowly roll up your spine, beginning at the base of your spine, one vertebra at a time.

Step 2: As you roll up, your head and neck stay dropped down and heavy.

Step 3: Let your shoulders fall into place, down and away from your ears.

Step 4: Feel your spine long and wide as you roll up. Slowly roll your head up. Feel your body standing in actor's neutral.

Step 5: Take a few steps and try to stay in neutral, letting your body move easily through space.

Breath

When we are born, our breath is natural. It supports and sustains us. A baby's natural breath is fluid and connected. A healthy baby uses the breath that is necessary to accomplish each new task that is learned. No more, no less. A healthy baby's voice, as it develops, can be heard very easily. In fact, it is often difficult NOT to hear a baby when she vocalizes (cry, scream, exclaim joy, etc.) A baby's breath assists each of her newly learned sounds. When a deeper breath is required, the body is ready and able to supply that support.

So why do actors need to "learn" to breathe? The process of releasing the natural breath has more to do with remembering than learning. As humans age, negative social, physical, and psychological influences create excess tension and obstruct the natural breath. These obstructions, or "blocks," limit an actor's ability to feel and use her breath effectively and efficiently.

Reconnecting with the natural breath may be easy for a beginning actor or it may be quite difficult. With patience and consistent work, however, anyone can do it.

Connecting with the Breath

Now that you are reacquainted with how your natural relaxed body feels, you are ready to begin the second step in the process of releasing your vocal instrument. That is, connecting with your breath. Continue to practice relaxation and alignment as you add this next step in the process of physical self-discovery. Relaxation and alignment is the foundation. Once you have a secure foundation, you can move on to the next level.

To understand the natural breathing process, it is helpful to observe children. It is most helpful to watch an infant. When she is at rest, her breathing can be seen in her entire body. An infant does not think about breathing, it happens naturally. When she emerges into this world from her mother's womb, her diaphragm expands and contracts involuntarily, and she takes her first breath. This first breath is often followed by some sound such as a whimper or a loud cry. Her parent(s) breathe their own sigh of relief. They are waiting for this sound. It means that their child has finally arrived. And like all baby mammals, their child must breathe to stay alive. The body certainly is amazing! No one teaches the baby to breathe. She instinctively knows how to do it. She has a primal, visceral knowledge that ensures her survival. If you watch a baby's body when she is at rest, you will notice her body in a completely relaxed state. In this state, you will notice that the baby's entire torso will expand and contract with each inhalation and exhalation. Her jaw is relaxed and dropped open. The air releases in through her nose, mouth, and throat and continues to move all the way down into the bottom of her torso. The sides of her torso will expand like a balloon as the breath releases in. Once her torso has expanded as much as is necessary to sustain her current needs, it will contract and the same air will release out through her mouth or nose. Watching the child, you can observe the "natural rhythm" of her breath. The air continually passes in and out. You can see the walls of the torso continually expanding and contracting. All of this action happens without control or conscious thought. The breath is there to sustain her life. If she is born healthy, there is no effort involved. The body is working according to its natural design.

This image of a relaxed, content baby is how you want to imagine yourself when you are beginning to reconnect with your natural rhythm of breathing. It may be difficult to do at first. You may want to "help" or control the breath. Get your mind out of it. Let go of control. Focus at first on relaxing and opening up your mouth, throat, and torso. Then focus on the movement of your torso.

Breathing Exercise #1: Connecting with the Breath in Neutral Supine

Step 1: Begin in neutral supine.

Step 2: Relax your body. Take yourself through one of the relaxation exercises in the section on relaxation.

Step 3: Feel your body. Let your body release into the pull of gravity.

Step 4: Let your jaw drop open. Feel an open yawning sensation in the back of your throat. Imagine that your mouth is a large open cave that feeds into the open empty elbow-shaped tube of your throat. This open empty tube then feeds down into the open empty chamber of your torso.

Step 5: Imagine that your torso (from your shoulders to your pelvis) is a very flexible open chamber. Imagine the breathing chamber of your torso is shaped like a soup can with walls made of a very flexible, soft, strong material like silk or elastic.

Step 6: Imagine the empty chamber of your torso expanding and contracting. As you feel the expansion, picture a balloon inflating or a parachute filling with air. Your body will expand and fill up as much as is required to fulfill your physical/vocal/emotional/spiritual needs at this time.

Step 7: Don't suck, push, or pull the air in. If you feel yourself controlling your inhalation as opposed to merely allowing the breath to release in, focus again on relaxation.

Step 8: Feel the expansion and contraction of your torso as you let the involuntary diaphragm muscle and all of the subtle muscles of the torso do what they are made to do—keep the rhythm of your breath moving.

Step 9: Think of breath as relaxation, power, and release. Trust that the amount of breath that your body and voice require will be there when you need it.

Breathing Exercise #2: The Six-Sided Box

Follow steps 1–4 of Breathing Exercise #1.

Step 1: Imagine the breathing chamber of your torso is shaped like a six-sided box made of a soft, flexible and strong material like silk or elastic.

Step 2: Feel the breath release into the TOP of the box. This side of the box is attached at your shoulders and can billow above your head like a parachute, as the breath releases in. It then floats back down as the breath releases out. Repeat until you can genuinely feel the movement in the top of the box. If you cannot feel the movement and begin to sense frustration or a need to "push" the breath, either go back to the relaxation stage and try again OR move on to another side of the box.

Step 3: Feel the breath release into the FRONT of the box. This side of the box is attached at your shoulders and pelvis. It may billow toward the ceiling like a parachute expanding up toward the ceiling as you lay on your back and the breath releases in. It then floats back down as the breath releases out. Repeat until you can feel the movement of the breath in the front of the box. If you cannot feel the movement and begin to sense frustration or a need to "push" the breath, either go back to the relaxation stage and try again OR move on to another side of the box.

Breathing into the TOP of the box

Step 4: Feel the breath release into the BOTTOM of the box. This side of the box is attached at your pelvis. It may billow down below your feet like a parachute, as the breath releases in. It then floats back up toward your pelvis as the breath releases out. Repeat until you can feel the movement in the bottom of the box. If you cannot feel

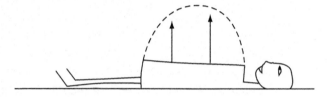

Breathing into the FRONT of the box

the movement and begin to sense frustration or a need to "push" the breath, either go back to the relaxation stage and try again OR move on to another side of the box.

Step 5: Let your right arm cross over your body to the left and roll onto your left side. Don't use your head and neck to turn. Keep your neck as relaxed as possible. Place your left hand under your head. Bend your right elbow toward the ceiling and place your RIGHT hand on the RIGHT side of your waist. (Your waist is the soft area between your last rib and your pelvis). Put your thumb toward your back and your fingers toward your abdomen and let the "web" of your hand rest fully on your RIGHT SIDE. Feel the breath release into the right side of the box. Let your side expand and billow up toward the ceiling as the breath releases in. The RIGHT SIDE floats back down toward your pelvis as the breath releases out. Repeat until you can feel the movement in the right side of the box. If you cannot feel the movement and begin to sense frustration or a need to "push" the breath, either go back to the relaxation stage and try again OR move on to another side of the box.

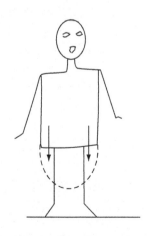

Breathing into the BOTTOM of the box

Step 6: Moving your arms and legs first, roll over onto your belly. Don't use your head and neck to turn. Keep your neck as relaxed as possible. Let the movement of the head and neck follow the movement of the arms, legs, and torso. Place your hands under your head, palms down and turn your face to the right or left side, whichever is more comfortable for you. Feel the breath release into the BACK of the box. This side

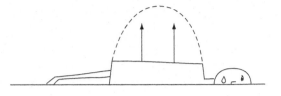

Breathing into the BACK of the box

of the box is attached at your back shoulders and your back pelvis. As the breath releases in, your BACK will billow and expand toward the ceiling like a parachute. The BACK floats back down as the breath releases out. Repeat until you can feel the movement in the front of the box. If you cannot feel the movement and begin to sense frustration or a need to "push" the breath, either go back to the relaxation stage and try again OR move on to another side of the box.

Step 7: Initiating the movement with your arms and legs, roll onto your right side into a fetal position. Don't use your head and neck to turn, keep your neck as relaxed as possible. Place your right hand under your head. Bend your LEFT elbow toward the ceiling and place your LEFT hand on your waist. Put your thumb toward your back and your fingers toward your abdomen and let the "web" of your hand rest fully on your LEFT SIDE. Feel the breath release into the left side of the box. Let your side expand and billow up

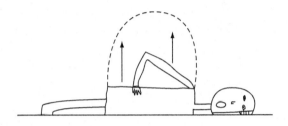

Breathing into the SIDE of the box

toward the ceiling as the breath releases in. The LEFT SIDE floats back down toward your pelvis as the breath releases out. Repeat until you can feel the movement in the LEFT SIDE of the box. If you cannot feel the movement and begin to sense frustration or a need to "push" the breath, either go back to the relaxation stage and try again OR move on to another side of the box.

Step 8: Using your arms and legs to initiate the movement, roll over onto your hands and knees.

Step 9: Keep your head and neck down, roll your toes under, bend your knees, push up into a dropped-down position.

Step 10: Slowly roll up your spine, beginning at the base of your spine, one vertebra at a time.

Step 11: Continue with Steps 26–30 of the Relaxation Visual Exercise on page 29.

Step 12: Take a few steps, stay in neutral, and let your body move easily through space. As you walk, feel the six-sided box expanding and contracting as the breath releases in and out.

Energy

Acting requires a great deal of physical, vocal, and emotional energy. A compelling and moving performance is dynamic. Without energy, a performance is lackluster and halfhearted. A dynamic performance will capture an audience's attention. A performance that lacks dynamism will leave an audience looking for something else. Their focus will not stay with the performance.

There are three types of energy that fuel an actor's performance: (1) Releasing an actor's natural energy; (2) Developing the vulnerability necessary to take in the energy an actor receives from his acting partner(s); and (3) Developing an awareness of the energy radiating from an audience and the ability to allow that energy to stimulate and invigorate a performance.

Releasing and Ordering the Actor's Natural Energy

A trained actor feels the energy that is within and emanates all around him. Ideally, an actor learns how to harness that energy so that he can make the best use of it in performance. An actor's body and voice use this channeled energy to respond in a way that is both natural and directed. This is a difficult balance to achieve. Without training, the actor's voice and body may resist. Energy that is not regulated is chaotic. In order to create art, an artist must learn to bring order to chaos.

The natural human body is efficient, flexible, strong, and dynamically responsive. Much of the work that must be done to sense and harness innate natural energy involves breaking down unnatural habits that the actor has developed. These habits cause his body to work ineffectively and inefficiently. This book explores the physical and cognitive elements that are involved in progressively training the actor's instrument. Once ineffective unnatural habits have been broken in one area, another is explored. New concepts and physical exercises are explored progressively, until the actor feels that his instrument is working with him. The training never ends. An actor is similar to an athlete. As long as he wants to play, he must practice for hours each day to keep himself ready for the "game" (i.e., performance). If this state is achieved and maintained, the actor will always be performance ready.

Vulnerability and Connecting with Your Partner's Energy

Ninety percent of acting is reacting. An actor takes in what his partner is doing and saying and reacts to it. In order to achieve this state, he must develop a strong sense of openness and vulnerability. To develop vulnerability, an actor allows his energy to flow toward his partner and allows his partner's energy to flow into himself. This exchange of energy happens instantaneously. Developing this type of exchange through vulnerability keeps the energy flowing in performance, and keeps things exciting. An actor never has time to "rest" during performance. He must be open and vulnerable, letting the energy flow into and out of himself.

> **Journal Exercise #19**
>
> *To be done after each of the above-mentioned breathing exercises.*
>
> - *Give a technical description of what the physical movement of your natural breath feels like. Use the names of body parts in your description (mouth, muscles, etc.) and be as specific as possible. Do not leave out any of the steps. Begin with, "When I breathe naturally, what happens is …"*
> - *Using a visual image, describe what your natural breathing feels like. Be as specific and detailed as possible in your description. Begin with "When I breathe naturally, I imagine that …"*

Without this exchange of energy, the performance will become stagnant. The energy needs to flow in the same way that the ocean waves flow in nature, creating unending drive, power, and dynamism.

Practicing the exercises in this book will help an actor to develop the vulnerability that will enable him to sustain this flow of energy.

Using the Audience's Energy

There is no performance without an audience. Knowing that you are being watched creates energy. Audiences emanate energy as they listen, sense, and feel along with the performers. The audience can feel the energy. The audience can build the energy. An actor is wise to allow the audience's energy to fuel his performance.

Flexibility, Strength, and Balance

Acting requires a great deal of flexibility, strength, and balance. An actor's body is trained to be supple, limber, powerful, and poised. Physical training enables the actor to achieve the demands of playing various types of characters. Once this training has been introduced, daily physical practice is required in order to maintain physical fluidity, strength, and balance.

An actor's voice is trained to be both pliant and resilient. It has the ability to express the widest range of emotions, tones, pitches, and dialects. For the stage actor, weeks of eight-hour rehearsals five to six days per week make great demands on his vocal instrument. The stage actor's voice must fill a large room for two to four hours at full volume almost every day of the week.

The mind and spirit of an actor must also be fluid, resilient, and balanced. Acting is hard work and it challenges a person's tenacity and inner strength. It is difficult to put yourself through the physical and emotional rigors of someone else's life and sustain equilibrium in your own. An actor feels—physically and emotionally—whatever his character is experiencing. Without training and hard work, this work can become exhausting and destructive to an actor's own psyche. He must learn to separate his life from the life of his character. Sometimes this is difficult. Actors have been known to become seriously depressed when playing an emotionally demanding role. Plays are not written about situations in life that are easy. Drama is conflict. Conflict is difficult—physically, vocally, emotionally, and spiritually.

This book's focus is primarily on stage acting, but students who want to be film actors should be aware that the demands are equally intense. A film or TV actor's day is often longer than that of a stage actor's. Some days they may shoot for 15 hours or more.

An actor must also learn how to take care of his body, voice, mind, and spirit. His art requires a great deal of him, physically, vocally, intellectually, and spiritually. If he is not taught how to properly care for his instrument—his body, mind, and spirit—he runs the risk of having a very short career and/or a very difficult life.

Some of the exercises and journal work in this book will begin to train an actor's spirit and mind to be flexible, strong, and balanced. They require interpersonal communication skills that will assist anyone in becoming more open and confident in his ability to connect with others. Journal work will assist an individual in understanding himself better and examining his strengths and weaknesses. Acknowledgment is often the first step a person takes to change his life in a positive way. However, I must offer the following word of caution to anyone who is looking for an acting class or an acting book to assist him in overcoming emotional or psychological issues.

Acting and Therapy

Some students will take acting classes to get in touch with their feelings. There is a misconception in the general population that acting is good "therapy." Many people think that an acting class can help people who have trouble identifying and/or expressing feelings.

It is true that many of the components of acting training will open a student up to emotional, physical, and spiritual parts of himself that have been repressed. However, acting training should not take the place of therapy. Most acting teachers are not trained therapists. Their ability to deal with emotional/psychological issues that may arise during a student's training process will depend a great deal on their level of sensitivity and experience with these issues. Generally, acting instructors do not have the expertise required to address a student's emotional/psychological issues. Credible acting teachers will suggest a student seek professional help from a trained therapist to deal with emotional/psychological issues that may arise.

There are trained therapists who use drama and other art forms as part of an individual's therapy. These classes should be labeled as "drama therapy" or "art therapy." A student, however, should not enter a "regular" acting class expecting therapy. And an acting teacher should not pose as a therapist, unless they have that specific training.

. . . .

Stretching Exercise to Increase Flexibility, Strength, and Balance.

Do this exercise on a yoga mat. Use a yoga brick if you are new to stretching and working on flexibility, strength, and balance.

Step 1: Lie on a mat in neutral supine. If you feel pain in your lower back when your legs are stretched out, bend your knees and put your feet flat on the floor until your lower back muscles begin to relax.

Step 2: Try to close your eyes. If closing your eyes makes you feel anxious or frightened, leave them open for now.

Step 3: Connect with your breath. Try to feel your breath in your lower abdomen. As the breath releases in, the abdomen rises. As the breath releases out, the abdomen falls. Feel your body. Empty your mind.

Step 4: Bend your knees and hug them into your chest.

Step 5: Put your hands on your knee caps. Keep your knees bent and legs together. Moving from the hips, circle your bent legs, moving first to the right, down, left, and up to the chest. This will help to loosen your hips and lower back. Circle the hips with the legs bent to the right AT LEAST five times. Finish with the bent knees pulled into the chest, legs together, and hands on the kneecaps. Circle your bent legs in the opposite direction, moving first to the left, down, right, and up to the chest. Circle the hips with the legs bent to the left AT LEAST five times. Finish with the bent knees pulled into the chest, legs together, and hands on the kneecaps.

Step 6: Stretch your arms out shoulder height on the mat, palms receiving the light from the ceiling. Release the breath in.

Step 7: Keeping your knees bent and legs together, let your legs drop toward your right elbow as you release the breath out. Let your head turn to the left. Feel the spine twisting as your upper and lower body turn in opposition to each other.

Step 8: As you release the breath in, while keeping the knees bent, bring your left leg to the center, followed by the right leg. Bring your head to the center.

Step 9: Keeping your knees bent and legs together, let your legs drop toward your left elbow as you release the breath out. Let your head turn to the right. Feel the spine twisting as your upper and lower body turn in opposition to each other.

Step 10: Release the breath in. Keeping the knees bent, bring your right leg to the center, followed by the left leg. Bring your head to the center.

Step 11: Continue on your own, side to side. Remember to breathe. Complete at least five repetitions on both sides, ending with your legs and head in the center of your body.

Step 12: Release the breath in. As you release the breath out, straighten your knees, and keeping the legs together, extend your legs straight up toward the ceiling. Flex your feet and spread your toes. (Use a yoga strap or tie around your calves if it is difficult to keep your legs straight when they are extended up to the ceiling.) Hold.

Step 13: Release the breath in. As you release the breath out, hug your knees into your chest. Release the breath in.

Step 14: As you release the breath out, let the legs release. Place the feet flat on the floor, keeping the knees bent.

Step 15: Interlace your fingers and place your palms under your head, with your thumbs released down along the back of your neck.

Step 16: Release the breath in. Using your core (abdomen) muscles, as you release the breath out, roll up onto your lower back. Bring your forehead up and look between your knees. Hold this position. Release the breath in and out, and breathe into your belly. See and feel the rise and fall of your breath. If your core feels strong enough, lift the feet off the mat and point the toes forward. Bring the hands to the side by the knees.

Step 17: Release the breath in. As you release the breath out, slowly roll back down onto the mat with control. Repeat this "roll up and hold" at least three times. Remember to breathe. Slowly roll down your spine onto your back. Feet are flat on the floor; knees are bent.

Step 18: Bring your arms back down by your sides, hands by your hips, palms receiving the light from the ceiling.

Step 19: Release the breath in. As you release the breath out, lift your buttocks off the ground as you push down into your feet and hands and lift your spine, balancing on your feet and your shoulders. Feel and see the rise and fall of your breath in your belly.

Step 20: Slide your hands under your lower back, interlace your fingers, and push your palms toward your feet and down into the floor simultaneously. Feel your chest opening and stretching toward the ceiling as your shoulder blades come closer together on your back.

Step 21: As you release the breath out, release your hands and let them come back by your hips. Slowly release your spine back down into the floor from the top to the base of the spine. Feel your spine as you release down one vertebra at a time. Release the breath in. As you release the breath out, repeat this pose at least three times.

Step 22: Hug your knees to your chest. Roll to your side into a fetal position.

Step 23: Roll over onto your front/belly and stretch your legs straight out behind you on the mat, with your toes pointed. Place your forehead on the mat.

Step 24: Slide your arms out in front of you, palms face down on the mat.

Step 25: Bend your elbows, slide your hands toward your body and place your hands flat on the mat by your ears.

Step 26: Release the breath in. As you release the breath out, push up with your arms and straighten your elbows.

Step 27: Keep your pelvis, legs, and thighs on the mat and look up toward the ceiling, arching your spine. Open your chest and feel your upper body reaching up toward the ceiling as your lower body pushes into the mat. If you feel pain in your lower back, let your upper body release closer to the mat and modify the arch in your lower back.

Step 28: Release the breath in. As you release the breath out, let your hands slide forward on the mat as you slowly release your upper torso down onto the mat.

Step 29: Repeat this movement at least three times. Remember to breathe.

Step 30: On a release of breath, push your torso up and back. Let your hips release back, placing your buttocks on your feet.

Step 31: Relax your neck and let your forehead rest on your stacked fists or on the mat and bring the arms by the sides, hands by the hips, palms receiving the light from the ceiling.

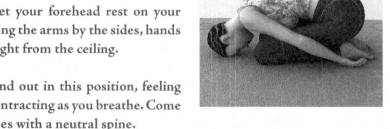

Step 32: Release the breath in and out in this position, feeling your lower back expanding and contracting as you breathe. Come forward onto your hands and knees with a neutral spine.

Step 33: As you release the breath in, feel the base of your spine and let your tailbone release down and back as the front your pelvis rolls toward the front of your body. Feel your spine stretch up like a parachute opening. Allow the middle of your back to release up toward the ceiling as your head drops down toward the floor.

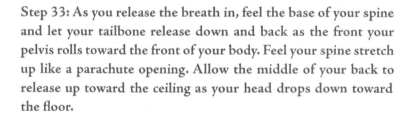

Step 34: As you release the breath out, feel the base of your spine and let your tailbone release up as your pelvis rolls down toward the floor, allowing the abdomen to release toward the floor as the chest releases forward and the forehead releases up toward the ceiling, arching the spine.

Step 35: Repeat this sequence of movements (cat and cow pose) at least five times, remembering to breathe.

Step 36: Come back to neutral spine (flat back). Place your hands directly under your shoulders. Make sure your hands are pushing flat down into the mat, feeling the weight on your palms, push your knuckles firmly into the mat. Let your head hang down.

Step 37: Curl your toes under. Release the breath in. As you release the breath out, push your hips straight up toward the ceiling and let your knees come off of the mat. Keep your knees bent. Feel the weight of your body balanced on your hands and your toes. Remember to breathe. Let your head and neck stay loose and released toward the ground.

Step 38: Straighten your legs and try to release your heels down to the floor. Continue to push up toward the ceiling through both your hands and legs. Remember to breathe. Let your head and neck stay loose and released toward the ground.

Step 39: Hold this position, feeling the relaxation of the breath and the strength required to hold the pose.

Step 40: Bring the right foot forward into a lunge. The knee should be over the ankle, not the toes, to reduce stress on the knee. Left leg is stretched out straight behind and the toes are curled under. Balance the weight evenly between the front and back foot. The hands are on either side of the right knee for balance. Lift the head and stretch the chest forward. Hold and breathe as you stretch.

Step 41: Bring the right foot back and push up into the downward-facing dog pose. Hold this position, feeling the relaxation of the breath and the strength required to hold the pose.

Step 42: Bring the left foot forward into a lunge pose. The knee should be over the ankle, not the toes, to reduce stress on the knee. The right leg is stretched straight out behind and the toes are curled under. Balance the weight evenly between the front and back foot. The hands are on either side of the left knee for balance. Lift the head and stretch the chest forward. Hold. Breathe.

Step 43: Bring the left foot back and push back to the downward-facing dog pose.

Step 44: Bend the knees and release onto the hands and knees, with a neutral spine.

Step 45: Release the buttocks down onto the feet (child's pose) and stretch the arms out in front of your body, palms on the mat. Crawl the fingers forward and feel the back stretch some more.

Step 46: Release the breath in. Release the breath out as you push the buttocks up into a dropped-down position.

Step 47: Place your hands on your thighs and bend your knees. Lift the head and chest toward the ceiling.

Step 48: Straighten your legs as you let your hands come out to your sides and over your head, bringing the palms together as you reach and stretch your whole body toward the ceiling.

Step 49: Bring the palms together to the chest.

Step 50: Turn the right foot out and the left foot in.

Step 51: Stretch the arms out, shoulder height, with the palms facing the floor. Turn the head to the right. Let the hips move to the left as you bend at the waist and release the right hand down to the right ankle (or a yoga brick). The left hand points upward toward the sky.

Step 52: Turn the head and look at the upper hand (triangle pose).

Step 53: Bend the right knee so that it is over the right ankle, keep the back leg extended out long and straight.

Step 54: Bend the left elbow and release the left arm over the left ear, palm facing down, left arm extended out to the right side. Hold the pose and breathe into the abdomen.

Step 55: Reach with your top arm, bend at the waist, and come up to a wide-stance forward pose, with both feet facing forward. Feel balance, strength, and focus in this pose.

Step 56: Turn the left foot out and the right foot in.

Step 57: Stretch the arms out, shoulder height, with the palms facing the floor, turn the head to the left. Let the hips move to the right as you bend at the waist and release the left hand to the left ankle (or a yoga brick). The right hand points up toward the sky.

Step 58: Turn the head and look at the upper hand (triangle pose).

Step 59: Bend the left knee so that the knee is over the left ankle; keep the back leg extended out long and straight.

Step 60: Bend the right elbow and release the right arm over the right ear, palm facing down, right arm extended out to the left side. Hold the pose and breathe into the abdomen.

Step 61: Reach with your top arm, bend at the waist, and come up to a wide-stance forward pose, with both feet facing forward. Place your hands on your hips and bend at the waist, keeping the legs straight, and release into a wide-stance forward bend with your hands placed on a brick or grabbing your ankles.

Step 62: Bring the legs a shoulder width apart and release into a dropped-down position. Slowly roll up your spine, beginning at the base of your spine, one vertebra at a time (spinal roll-up).

Step 63: Take a few steps and try to stay in neutral, letting your body move easily through space.

. . . .

Open response journal entry #20

Write in your journal using the following prompts. Respond in detail.

- *Right now I physically feel …*
- *Right now I emotionally feel …*
- *When I compare my body to how it felt before I began this exercise, it feels …*
- *During the exercise I was thinking about …*
- *During the exercise I imagined …*
- *The parts of my body that I could not feel were …*
- *I noticed the flexibility in …*
- *I felt strong when …*
- *I felt balanced when …*
- *The physical and/or emotional things that surprised me as I began to notice my flexibility, strength, and balance were …*
- *Flexibility is …*
- *Strength is …*
- *Balance is …*

Resonance

Now that you have begun to connect with your relaxed natural body and the natural rhythm of your breath, it is time to make some noise and focus more specifically on vocal training. Vocal training involves retraining the voice to release sound in a healthy and emotionally connected way. Once the actor's body is relaxed and her breath is flowing naturally, she can begin to explore sound.

It is important that when an actor speaks, she is heard. How is she heard? Resonance! Resonance is the vibration that is felt when sound is added to breath. If we think of our voice as a musical instrument, the resonance, or vibration, is what gives it power and volume. The resonance of the voice can also affect your acting partner and audience members emotionally. When you resonate, you are making molecules of sound bounce around. They bounce inside of you (interior resonance) and outside of you (exterior resonance). The texture and shape of these resonating molecules can bounce off your partner to soothe, to incite, to terrify, etc. It is with resonance that we move our voice to the outside and begin to affect others. It is with resonance that we begin "acting" with sound as well as movement.

· ·

Resonance Exercise

Step 1: Begin in neutral supine. Use one of the aforementioned breathing exercises to connect with the breath.

Step 2: Imagine that there is a pool of vibrations in the bottom of the torso.

Step 3: Release the breath in through your open mouth and throat. Let the breath pick up the vibrations from the torso and release the stream of vibration onto the roof of the mouth. The soft palate is relaxed and open.

Step 4: The resultant sound you will hear will be an open "ah" sound. Release all of the breath on sound.

Step 5: Keep the mouth open and release another breath down into the pool of vibrations. Gently touch your lips together, keeping your jaw relaxed and open.

Step 6: Release the stream of vibrations onto the lips, feeling the vibrations on the lips (lip hum). Feel free to move the lips around as you hum, letting the hum move around on the lips. Release the jaw and mouth open, and allow the breath to release down into the pool of vibrations. Repeat the lip hum until you feel a rich sense of vibration on your lips (lip hum).

Step 7: Repeat the lip hum a number of times, sensing the resonance on the lips and in the "mask" area of the front of the face (cheeks and nose).

Step 8: The face may feel tingly and itchy as the face muscles continue to relax and loosen as the sound vibrates on the front of the face.

Step 9: When you feel as if you need breath, release the jaw and mouth open and allow the breath to release down into the pool of vibrations.

Step 10: Release a stream of vibrations with the lips together and the mouth open as if it is full of something you have just eaten that is relatively large, crunchy, and juicy, like an apple or a pear.

Step 11: Let the vibrations move around in the mouth as you chew, moving the mouth up and down and keeping the lips together (chew hum). Repeat the chew hum a number of times, sensing the resonance on the lips, in the "mask" area of the front of the face and in the mouth. The face and mouth may feel tingly and itchy as the face and mouth muscles continue to relax and loosen, as the sound vibrates on the front of the face and in the mouth.

Step 12: When you feel as if you need breath, release the jaw and mouth open and allow the breath to release down into the pool of vibrations. Release a stream of vibrations with the lips together, the mouth stretched long, the soft palate stretched open in the back of the throat, and the tongue resting on the bottom of the mouth.

Step 13: Let the vibrations move around in the mouth and skull as you stretch the soft palate open, mouth stretched long, and the lips together (yawn hum). Repeat the yawn hum a number of times, feeling the resonance in the "mask" area of the front of the face (cheeks, nose), the mouth and skull, and on the lips. The face, mouth, lips, and skull may feel tingly and itchy as noted in the lip and chew hum. The sound may feel like a bell tolling in the top of your skull.

Step 14: When you feel as if you need breath, release the jaw and mouth open and allow the breath to release down into the pool of vibrations. Repeat the hum that you feel is most resonant for you. Establish the stream of vibrations with the hum and drop your jaw open to an "ah." Make sure your soft palate is lifted in the back and your tongue is relaxed on the bottom of your mouth.

Step 15: Continue to connect with the breath; initiate and release the hum on "ah" as you roll onto your right side. Keep your head and neck relaxed.

Step 16: Initiate and release the hum to "ah" as you curl up into a fetal position and then over onto your hands and knees. Keep your head and neck down. Initiate and release the hum to "ah" as you bend your knees, then move into a dropped-down position.

Step 17: When you need breath, release the breath in. Establish the hum and release on "ah" as you continue to roll up. Take your time.

Step 18: Release a number of lip, chew, and yawn hums to "ah" while moving your body around (jump up and down, bounce your shoulders, shake your buttocks, drop down your spine, roll up your spine, etc.) Focus on feeling the resonance move as your body moves.

Step 19: Come back to actor's neutral.

....

Articulation

Articulation is the formation of clear and distinct sounds in speech. On the most basic level, an actor needs to have good articulation so that she can be understood by her acting partner(s) and the audience. Clear articulation enables a performer to distinctly communicate her character's thoughts and feelings. The articulators are muscles that must be trained in order to respond quickly, with clarity and with accuracy. The articulators include the lips, the tongue, and the soft palate. If any of the articulators are lazy or flaccid, it will affect the clarity of the actor's speech and may render her incomprehensible at times. Training the articulators requires a good deal of practice and repetition.

Articulation deals with the two types of sounds that make up language: consonants and vowels. This book will deal with Standard American English, and thus the vowels and consonants that are found in it. If an actor is playing a character with a dialect, the formation of these sounds may vary. However, once an actor has "tuned up" the articulators, he can "feel" the sounds he makes with his voice. Learning a new dialect becomes a matter of adjusting how sounds are made with certain articulators or placing primary resonance in a new part of the face, throat, or mouth.

Vowels and Emotion

Most raw emotions are expressed with open vowel sounds. When we feel pleasure, pain, excitement, satisfaction, fear, etc., the sounds that are released are vowel sounds: "oh," "ow," "oo," "ah," "ee," "ay," "i," and "ahyee." Vowels are released with a relaxed jaw, and various levels of open space in the mouth. The openness of vowels enables the sound to come forward into the mouth and resonate fully. Babies and children make very open and resonant vowel sounds—the natural sounds of emotional expression. The making of open, resonant, rich vowels is a skill with which most humans are born. When people experience extreme emotions, they may find the true unrefined expression of these vowel sounds once again. However, in everyday speech, most adults tend to "shorthand" or limit the duration of vowel sounds. This—like other limitations created through learned tension—inhibits the truthful and complete expression of emotions. Speech becomes controlled, the jaw becomes locked or stiff, and vowels lose much of their power to express.

In order to reawaken the ability to spontaneously and fully express her emotional life, an actor must retrain her body to give the emotional sounds of vowels the space and shape they need.

The first tasks are to relax the jaw, open the mouth, open the throat, relax the tongue, and use the breath on sound.

....

Jaw Relaxation Exercise

Step 1: Begin with a relaxation exercise. Connect with the breath and warm up the voice with one of the resonance exercises. Once you can feel your relaxed and resonant voice fully supported by breath, work on relaxing the jaw.

Step 2: Gently clench your teeth together and find your jaw hinge muscle with your fingers. (When you clench your teeth, the jaw hinge muscle will protrude on the sides of the face.) Keep your fingers on that area of your cheek and relax the jaw by letting it hang as loosely as possible.

Step 3: Massage the jaw hinge muscle with a circular motion.

Step 4: Massage the jaw hinge muscle by kneading into the muscle with the fingertips.

Step 5: Loosen the jaw hinge muscle by drawing straight down with the fingers from the top jaw to the base of the bottom jaw.

Step 5: Once the jaw feels relaxed, practice shaking the jaw up and down. Grab the lower jaw with the thumbs underneath and the index fingers on top.

Step 6: Imagine that your jaw is loose and hanging down—like it would be on a science room skeleton if the skeleton did not have something (an elastic) holding the lower jaw up.

Step 7: Shake the jaw down and then let it release up (don't push it up).

Step 8: Make sure your hands are doing the shaking and you are not using your jaw muscles to move the jaw up and down. Don't push the jaw up. If your teeth "click" together, you are either pushing the jaw up or using your jaw muscle to pull the lower jaw up. Massage the jaw again; let it relax.

Step 9: Make a fist with your thumbs inside your fingers and place your thumb knuckles into the crease in your chin, below your teeth where the lower jawbone begins.

Step 10: Relax the jaw open and push it down and back with your knuckles. Let the jaw spring back up; do not push it up.

Open response journal entry #22

Write in your journal using the following prompts. Respond in detail.

- *When I massage and release my jaw, I physically feel ...*
- *When I massage and release my jaw, I emotionally feel ...*
- *When I compare my jaw now to how it felt before I began this exercise, it feels ...*
- *During the exercise I was thinking about ...*
- *During the exercise I imagined my jaw ...*

Relaxing the jaw entails a degree of "mind over matter." It takes times and practice. If your jaw does not seem to be moving and you are getting frustrated, leave this exercise and do something else. Come back to it later when you are more relaxed. The more you massage, relax, and practice loosening the jaw in your everyday life, the more it will release. Allow yourself to let your jaw hang open throughout the day. Check in during stressful times during your day and notice if your jaw is clenched. If it is, consciously let it go and massage your jaw hinge muscle a bit. You are retraining your jaw to relax and hang open—in the same way that a baby or small child's jaw hangs open when he is relaxed.

Once the jaw is relaxed, begin loosening up your lips.

Lip Loosening Exercise

Step 11: Stretch the lips from side to side with the fingers & blow through.

Step 12: Gently pull the top and bottom lips forward with your hands in a "praying position" and then let them release and spring back.

Step 13: Purse the lips forward making an exaggerated "oo" sound then stretch them back making an exaggerated "ee" sound. Repeat.

Step 14: Stretch the lips and blow through on sound, release to an "ah." Repeat the "ah," keep the jaw relaxed, and purse the lips forward to an "oo."

Step 15: Continue, keeping the jaw relaxed and the lips active, creating the following vowel sounds, finding an emotional image that connects with each vowel sound.

Step 16: Work for maximum oral space on the open vowels. These are labeled "open." Work for very active lip activity on those vowels that are labeled "active lips." Some of the vowel sounds combine the open space with the active lips. These are labeled accordingly. Strive for a relaxed jaw, open throat, and active lips to create resonant vowel sounds.

Step 17: "ah" (pleasure, etc.)—OPEN.

Step 18: "oo" (satisfaction, etc.)—ACTIVE LIPS—stretched forward to create the smallest lip opening; sound resonates on the lips.

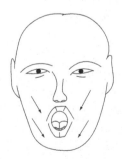
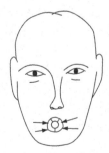
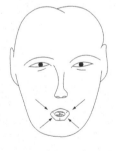
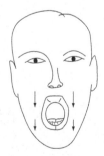
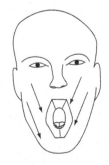

Ah lip formation. As in far, card, shark.

OO lip formation.

Ee lip formation. As in sleep, keep, heap, cheap.

Uh lip formation. As in cup, pup, supper.

Aw lip formation. As in law, awful, maul.

Step 19: "ee" (joy, etc.)—ACTIVE LIPS—lips pursed forward, sound resonates on the hard palate and lips.

Step 20: "oh" (contentment, etc.)—Long open to active pursed-forward lips, resonance moves from hard palate to lips.

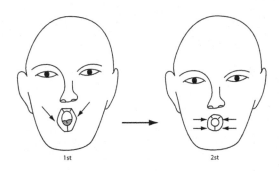

O lip formation. As in go, no, so, blow, toe.

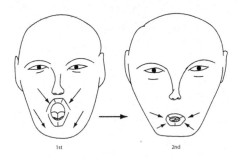

Ah-yee lip formation. As in kite, night, write, sight.

Step 21: "uh" (perseverance, etc.)—DROP JAW.

Step 22: "aw" (disappointment, etc.)—LONG, OPEN LIPS.

Step 23: "ahyee" (long I sound) (surprise, etc.)—COMBINATION—OPEN to lips pursed forward, sound resonates on the hard palate and lips.

Step 24: "ah-oo" (ow sound) (pain, etc.)—COMBINATION—OPEN to stretched forward to create the smallest opening; resonance moves from the hard palate to the lips.

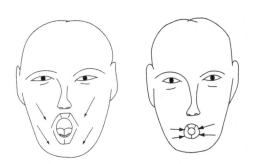

Ah-oo lip formation.

Consonants and Clarity

Consonants are used in language for vocal clarity and to punctuate or accentuate. Consonants can be hard or soft. They are used in words to communicate meaning through intellectual understanding and the impact the sound has on the receiver of the information. Clear, effortless speech is a necessity for an actor. The articulators must be exercised regularly so they can make sounds with speed and precision. The three articulators that need to be tuned are the lips, the tongue, and the soft palate.

. . . .

Exercises/Warm-Up for Articulation

The Lips

Step 1: Relax the body, connect to the breath, relax the jaw. Once the jaw is relaxed, begin loosening up your lips.

Step 2: Stretch the lips from side to side with the fingers and blow through.

Step 3: Gently pull the top and bottom lips forward with your hands in a "praying position," and then let them release and spring back.

Step 4: Purse the lips forward and make an "oo" sound; then stretch them back and produce an "ee" sound. Repeat. Stretch the lips and blow through on sound; release to an "ah" using very active lips.

Step 5: Feeling your voice vibrating on your lips as you blow through, release to a vowel sound and then produce the lip consonant sounds listed below. Repeat each lip consonant/vowel sound combination at least three times. Do a number of these repetitions until your lips are feeling very alive and vibrant.

Example: Blow through on the lips, release to "oo," and then add the lip consonant "w" to create "woo, woo, woo" (repeat several times).

Lip consonant sounds: P, W, B, M.

> *Open response journal entry #24*
>
> *Write in your journal using the following prompts. Respond in detail.*
>
> * *Focusing on lip formation while keeping my jaw relaxed made me aware of ...*
> * *The lip consonants that are difficult for me to feel and form are ...*
> * *The lip consonants that are easy for me to form and feel in my mouth are ...*

Step 1: Relax the body, connect to your breath, and relax the jaw.

Step 2: Massage the base of the tongue. (See number 10 in diagram.) Place the thumbs underneath the chin. Pushing gently, move around the muscle under the chin and above the neck.

Step 3: Relax the jaw open.

Step 4: Place the tip of the tongue on the back of the bottom teeth. Let the tongue stretch forward and imagine that the base of the tongue can roll out of the mouth, with the tip pressed firmly against the back of the bottom teeth. This stretch will push the jaw wide open.

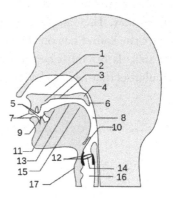

NOTE: As you practice the following tongue stretches, stretch the tongue out and release it back slowly in order to achieve maximum stretch. If you stretch too quickly, the tongue will stretch to the same point each time.

Step 5: Hold the tongue in this stretched position and take a few deep breaths. Don't move the tongue when you breathe, keep it stretched forward. Picture the breath releasing in and out OVER the tongue as you breathe.

Step 6: VERY slowly, release the tongue back into the mouth, letting the jaw slowly release out of its wide-open stretch at the same time.

Step 7: Repeat this tongue stretch AT LEAST three times. Remember to go slowly on both the stretch and the release.

Step 8: After completing the tongue stretches, let the tongue lie on the bottom of the mouth, resting the tip of the tongue against the back of the bottom teeth.

Step 9: Keep the jaw relaxed and bring the lips together.

Step 10: Bring the tongue forward onto the inside of the top lip.

Step 11: Let the tongue trace the inside of the lips in a circular motion. Keep the lips together.

Step 12: Circle the tongue to the right three or four times and then to the left three or four times, repeat this sequence three times.

Step 13: Relax the jaw and tongue.

Step 14: Push the tongue to the middle of the inside right cheek. Keep the lips together and the jaw relaxed and inactive. Push the right cheek out with the tongue.

Step 15: Push the tongue to the middle of the inside left cheek. Keep the lips together and the jaw relaxed and inactive. Push the left cheek out with the tongue.

Step 16: Repeat Steps 13 and 14 six or seven times, moving the tongue from side to side and pushing out the cheeks with the tongue. Keep the lips together and the jaw relaxed and inactive.

Step 17: Relax the jaw open and let the tongue rest on the roof of the mouth and blow sound through onto the roof of the mouth. Allow the relaxed tongue to vibrate on the roof of the mouth (the resultant sound is a "trill" or "rolled 'r'" sound.)

Step 18: Feel the voice vibrate on the tongue and roof of the mouth as you trill on voiced sound. Release the jaw open to an open vowel sound. Let the tongue drop down to the bottom of the mouth as you release on the open vowel sound and then produce the tongue consonant sounds listed below. Repeat each vowel/tongue consonant combination at least three times. Do a number of these repetitions until your tongue is feeling very alive and vibrant.

Example: Trill on the tongue and roof of the mouth. Release to "ah," and then add the tongue consonant "t" to create "tah, tah, tah" (repeat several times).

Tongue consonant sounds: T, L, N, D, S, Z.

> *Open response journal entry #25*
> _____
> *Write in your journal using the following prompts. Respond in detail.*
>
> - *Focusing on using my tongue to make consonant sounds while keeping my jaw relaxed made me aware of ...*
> - *The tongue consonants that are difficult for me to feel and form are ...*
> - *The tongue consonants that are easy for me to form and feel are ...*

The Soft Palate

Step 1: Relax the body, connect to your breath, and relax the jaw.

Step 2: Yawn your mouth open, stretching your soft palate in the back of your throat. Bring your tongue forward so that it is lying on the bottom of your mouth and the tongue tip is on the back of the bottom teeth. Repeat this yawn stretch at least five times.

Open response journal entry #26

Write in your journal using the following prompts. Respond in detail.

- Focusing on using my soft palate to make consonant sounds while keeping my jaw relaxed made me aware of ...
- The soft palate consonants that are difficult for me to feel and form are ...
- The soft palate consonants that are easy for me to form and feel are ...

Step 3: Establish a stream of vibrations with a lip, chew, or yawn hum. Drop your jaw open to a vowel sound. Feel the vibrations moving into the soft palate as they move up and down in the back of the throat on the soft palate consonant sounds.

Step 4: Repeat each vowel/soft palate consonant sound combination at least three times. Do a number of these repetitions until your soft palate is feeling very alive and vibrant.

Example: Initiate the hum. Release to "oh" and then add the soft palate consonant "g" to create "goh, goh, goh" (repeat several times).

Soft Palate Consonant Sounds: G, K , NG, H.

Finish off with tongue twisters to practice combining vowel formation with lip, tongue, and soft palate consonant formation.

....

Tongue Twisters

Work slowly at first, and then pick up speed. Work for optimal oral space, minimum involvement of the jaw, and maximum activity of the articulators. REMEMBER TO FOCUS ON HOW THE LIPS, TONGUE, AND SOFT PALATE FEEL as they resonate. KEEP THE JAW RELAXED AS MUCH AS POSSIBLE. Do not listen to yourself speak—this will only slow you down.

1. Paula's intensely specific party planning pooped her out.
2. Let me listlessly lower the large long liquid lava lamp.
3. Ginormous gray gargoyles gain grains of grime from age to age.
4. Dave dug difficult drains in the dank and dirty dungeon.
5. Ting and Tang tried and tried to test the ticking clock's ticking tock.
6. Barbara bent big black bars behind the broad birch bench.
7. Kai colored Kiernan's clever candy wrapper creation.
8. Unique New York neophytes never perform punctilious injunctions.

The Dynamics

The way in which an individual moves can communicate a great deal about that person's life. The manner in which someone's body interacts with the forces of gravity and the space that surrounds him may reveal much about his character, temperament, history, status, and life experiences.

Individuals have a natural rhythm and a developed rhythm. A person's natural rhythm is the rhythm with which he is born. At birth, each child seems to have an innate rhythm. The rate at which his daily life flows has a natural tempo that fits his personality. As a child grows, many factors influence how his daily rhythm might alter. He may adapt his natural rhythm in certain circumstances as life events have an impact on him physically, emotionally and spiritually. This rhythm is his developed rhythm.

An actor must learn to identify his own rhythm—both natural and developed. He then can learn to how to adjust his rhythm and explore rhythms of other people. This process of exploration requires quite a bit of the actor. It asks that he play and use his imagination the way a child does. It compels the actor to let go of his inhibitions and fear of looking silly. And it requires the actor to push himself physically, if the type of movement he is asked to explore is unfamiliar to him.

One way for an actor to explore different rhythms and types of movement is through exploring the body's dynamics. The dynamics are explored by Michael Chekhov in his book *To the Actor*.[1] The following exercises introduce the actor to the basics of this aspect of Chekhov's approach to movement for the actor.

The four physical dynamics that we will practice are floating, flying, pressing, and thrusting.

Learning Points

1: Each time this warm-up is practiced, the actor should push herself to explore new ways in which to move her body. At first, she may be inclined to move primarily her arms. Once she begins to move about the room, she may always leave her feet firmly planted on the ground. Encourage her to use her ENTIRE body to move in each dynamic. Ask her to be aware of and trust the flexibility, strength, and balance she possesses.

2: If she becomes tired, any of the dynamics can be done from a sitting or lying-down position. The goal is to move the body continuously while connecting to the image. Allow the image to affect the tempo, quality, fluidity, strength, etc., of the body.

3: The Dynamics warm-up is practiced with music. Some suggestions have been given, but the actor is encouraged to include new choices that inspire her.

---

1   Chekhov, Michael. *To the Actor: On the Technique of Acting*. Rutledge Publishing, Inc. 2002.

Dynamics Warm-Up

This exercise is done on a gym mat of medium thickness. Begin by exploring one dynamic for a good deal of time. Add a new dynamic each day, until you can explore all four Dynamics in one warm-up. Move from one dynamic to the next, always beginning and ending with the floating dynamic. Prepare with a stretching warm-up.

Step 1: Lie on the floor in actor's neutral. Feel the ebb and flow of your breath as it releases in and out of your body. Feel your body.

Step 2: Feel the flow of energy in your body. Try to let go of excess tensions and inhibitions.

Floating

"Begin floating music" [2]

Step 1: Create an image in your mind of something floating through the air (a feather, a cloud, a helium balloon, an astronaut floating in space ...). Create the image in your mind's eye as clearly and specifically as possible.

Step 2: On an intake of breath, let one arm begin to float up off the mat. The movement is slow, soft, light, and gentle. Continue to breathe and move the arm, using as much space as possible.

Step 3: Add the other arm, letting both arms float through the air, as if they are not bound by gravity. Let the arms slowly float back down to the mat.

Step 4: Let one leg float up off the mat and then the other. Let the legs release from the mat as if they are not bound by the pull of gravity. Remember to breathe. Use as much space as possible.

Step 5: As the legs float, allow the torso to follow as if there is no gravity.

Step 6: Float over onto your belly.

Step 7: Let all the parts of your body float up off the mat. Allow your body to float around the room.

Step 8: Explore floating up and floating down. Remember to keep the movements slow, light, soft, and gentle.

---

2   Hilary Stagg, *Feather Light*, Real Music, 1989.; Haydn, CELLO 1, Adagio; Haydn, CELLO 2, Adagio; John Barry, *Dances with Wolves Soundtrack*, "Two Socks—The Wolf Theme," TIG Productions, 1990.

Step 9: This movement will allow you to explore and enhance your strength and ability to balance. This movement looks easy and slow, but it requires a good deal of strength to move slowly and gently with all parts of your body.

Step 10: Use your breath to keep your muscles fueled with energy. If you hold your breath, your muscles will be stressed and you will tire more easily.

Step 11: Explore floating movements with your whole body on and off the mat.

Step 12: Slowly float back to the mat and float back to a neutral supine position.

Step 13: Feel your body. Notice the rhythm of your breath, notice how you feel physically, and how you feel emotionally.

Flying

"Begin flying music" [3]

Step 1: Create an image in your mind of something flying through the air (an arrow shot from a bow, a rocket being launched, a bird of prey attacking …). Create the image in your mind's eye as clearly and specifically as possible.

Step 2: On an intake of breath, let one arm begin to fly up off the mat. The movement is quick, light, and energized. Continue to breathe and move the arm, using as much space as possible.

Step 3: Add the other arm, letting both arms fly through the air.

Step 4: Let the energy of the arms fly the torso up into a sitting position. Let the torso and arms fly as you remain on the mat.

Step 5: Let the energy of the arms and torso "fly" the lower part of the body, first onto the knees, then onto the feet. Remember to breathe.

Step 6: Allow all parts of your body to fly around the room. Use as much space as possible. Explore flying up and down.

Step 7: Remember to keep the movements energized and fast. Imagine that you can fly.

Step 8: Jump up as high as you can. As you fly, think "up," and allow your whole body to follow this command.

---

3   John Williams. *Harry Potter and the Sorcerer's Stone.* "The Quidditch Match," Warner Brothers. 2001.; *E.T. The Extra-Terrestrial.* "The Magic of Halloween," Geffen Records. 1982; Haydn, Cello –Concerto No. 1, Allegro; Mozart, *The Marriage of Figaro.*

Step 9: If you are relying too much on your arms and the idea of "wings," relax the arms and lead with another part of your body (your head, your chest, your toes ...).

Step 10: This movement will allow you to explore and enhance your strength, balance, and stamina.

Step 11: Have fun and allow yourself to be a child again.

Step 12: Use the mats and do the following sequence, listening to your body and what feels safe: run, jump high, roll on the mat, and fly back up again. Repeat this sequence a few times.

Step 13: Use your breath to keep your muscles fueled with energy. If you hold your breath, your muscles will be stressed and you will tire more easily.

Step 14: Explore flying movements with your whole body, on and off the mat.

Step 15: Be conscious of those who are around you. Allow yourself freedom without being reckless and inconsiderate of your classmates.

Step 16: If you tire, fly to the mat and work on your back, stomach, or knees, using flying movement.

Step 17: When you are ready, move off the mat again.

"Begin floating music"

Step 18: Slow down your movements to floating—gentle, soft, light, slow movements.

Step 19: Feel the change in your body as you move from flying to floating.

Step 20: Slowly float back to the mat and to a neutral supine position.

Step 21: Feel your body: Notice the rhythm of your breath, notice how you feel physically and emotionally.

Pressing

"Begin pressing music" [4]

Step 1: Create an image in your mind of something very forceful and/or heavy pressing on all parts of your body (walls of heavy stone pushing down and in on you, a hurricane force wind

---

4   John Barry. *Dances with Wolves* Soundtrack. "The Death of Timmons" or "Pawnee Attack." TIG Productions. 1990; John Williams. *Harry Potter and the Sorcerer's Stone*, "The Chess Game," Warner Bros. 2001.

pressing on you in every direction, a great wall of water or powerful wave …). Create the image in your mind's eye as clearly and specifically as possible.

Step 2: On an intake of breath, let one arm begin to press up off the mat. The movement is slow, slight, labored, and requires a great deal of imagination. Continue to breathe and move the arm up, "pressing" against the imaginary force. Relax your face and neck. Add the other arm, letting both arms press. Remember to breathe.

Step 3: The instructor can now circulate around the room and push back on the student's arms, which should be difficult to press down. Encourage the student to press against the resistance.

Step 4: The instructor should make the student aware of when she is going to release and move on, so that he can continue to work with his imagination when she releases the resistance.

Step 5: Allow all the parts of your body to press up off the mat. Become aware of what parts of your body are the strongest, and press those parts into a position that will allow you to have some leverage and a strong foundation. Keep the movements slow, strong, slight, and labored.

Step 6: As you become tired, clarify the specifics of the image and believe in it. Allow yourself to be a child again and pretend that the tremendous force and pressure is real.

Step 7: Press yourself over so that you are on your hands and knees or your stomach. Find a point across the room that you need to get to and begin to press your body in that direction. Feel the resistance pressing on you in every direction.

Step 8: Press yourself up a bit higher and continue to move against the resistance.

Step 9: The instructor may stop the music for a second or make a loud noise to signal that the pressure is released. The student will let his body react to this, and imagine that the pressure resumes again within three seconds (the instructor can cue this or the student can do it himself).

Step 10: Continue this sequence of resistance/release for five or six repetitions.

Step 11: Use your breath to keep your muscles fueled with energy. If you hold your breath, your muscles will be stressed and you will tire more easily. Continue to press toward the desired point across the room.

"Begin floating music"

Step 12: Slow down your movements to floating—gentle, soft, slow, light movements.

Step 13: Feel the change in your body as you move from pressing to floating.

Step 14: Slowly float back to the mat to a neutral supine position.

Step 15: Feel your body, notice the rhythm of your breath, notice how you feel physically and emotionally.

Thrusting

"Begin thrusting music"[5]

Step 1: Picture all of the joints in your body, and sense the great mobility these joints give you.

Step 2: You have many movable parts in your: neck, shoulders, elbows, wrists, hands, fingers, spine, hips, pelvis, knees, ankles, feet, and toes.

Step 3: Thrusting is exploring these movable parts and moving beyond the limitations you have imposed on yourself.

Step 4: Create an image in your mind of something making a thrusting motion (a fencing sword hitting its mark, a machine or robot moving, a break dancer …). Create the image in your mind's eye as clearly and specifically as possible.

Step 5: On an intake of breath, begin to thrust with your fingers. The movement is fast, short, sharp, and forceful.

Step 6: Thrust your arms off the mat. Continue to breathe and thrust the arms, using as much flexibility in the joints as possible.

Step 7: Thrust the torso up into a sitting position. Let the torso, arms, and legs thrust as you move on the mat.

Step 8: Let the energy of the arms, torso, and legs thrust the lower part of the body, first onto the knees then onto the feet. Remember to breathe.

Step 9: Thrust as you move around the room, using different parts of your body and as much space as possible. Explore thrusting up, down, forward, backward, diagonally, and from side to side. Remember to keep the movements short, sharp, and forceful.

---

5   Andreas Vollenweider. *Dancing with the Lion.* Sony Music. 1989; Brent Lewis. *Drum Sex,* "Needy, Needy, Needy." 2004; Deep Forest. "Karanga Beat," "M'ganga's Devotion."

Step 10: Have fun and allow yourself to move parts of your body that you may not move regularly (pelvis, hips, rib cage).

Step 11: Use your breath to keep your muscles fueled with energy.

Step 12: Remain in one location and thrust. Explore big thrusting and very small, precise thrusting.

Step 13: If you tire, thrust to the mat and work on your back, stomach, or knees, using thrusting movements.

Step 14: When you are ready, move off the mat again.

"Begin floating music"

Step 15: Slow down your movements to floating—gentle, soft, light, slow movements.

Step 16: Slowly float back to the mat and down to a neutral supine position.

Step 17: Feel your body, notice the rhythm of your breath, notice how you feel physically and emotionally.

••

Open response journal entry #27

Complete these journal entries after experiencing each of the dynamics. This reflective writing will promote understanding of how movement affects the whole actor—body, mind, and spirit.

- *The image I used for floating (flying, pressing, thrusting) was ...*
- *While I was floating (flying, pressing, thrusting) the physical sensations that I felt in my body were ...*
- *While I was floating (flying, pressing, thrusting), the emotions I felt were ...*
- *While I was floating (flying, pressing, thrusting), some of the images that came into my mind were ...*
- *I feel comfortable floating (flying, pressing, thrusting) these parts of my body ...*
- *I DO NOT feel comfortable floating (flying, pressing, thrusting) these parts of my body ...*
- *As I was floating (flying, pressing, thrusting) and I had to balance, I felt ...*
- *After I finished floating (flying, pressing, thrusting), I physically felt ...*
- *After I finished floating (flying, pressing, thrusting), I emotionally felt ...*
- *I do/do not like floating (flying, pressing, thrusting) because ...*

Part 2
Beginning to Act

Chapter 3
Creating with Others
Physical and Vocal Improvisation

Starting to Act

Your body and voice have started to free up again. You are ready to use them to begin practicing the art of acting. You've done the physical, vocal, intellectual, and spiritual work to allow your instrument to connect to the freedom of truthful, honest expression. It is now time to use your instrument in a focused way to DO something. That is what acting is—it is doing. The root of the word acting is ACT—and to ACT means to do.

Vulnerability Is Strength

Up until this point, this text has focused primarily on physically freeing the actor's instrument. The work will now move to working primarily with—and off of—other people. The people you will work with are your acting partners and/or ensemble members. It is critical that an actor allow herself to be vulnerable when she is working with her partner(s). It takes courage to be vulnerable. Many adults are afraid of vulnerability. When I approach the subject of vulnerability in my classes, some students resist:

Teacher: In order to be a good actor, you need to allow yourself to be vulnerable. Vulnerability is strength.

Student A: How can that be?

Student B: Vulnerability means weakness.

Teacher: Why do you think vulnerability is weakness?

Student B: People who are weak and can be hurt are vulnerable. That's a bad thing. I don't want to be vulnerable.

Teacher: So you think that, if you are strong, you never get hurt?

Student B: Well, yeah … but …

Student C: I think what she's trying to say is that everyone gets hurt. Right?

Teacher: Yes, sometimes we do. Sometimes things happen to us that hurt. However, we never know what is going to happen, correct? If we don't allow ourselves to be open and vulnerable, we may prevent some of the bad things from happening to us, but we will also miss out on a lot of great things that might happen. The thing about the armor that we put on to protect ourselves is that it is not selective. If we close ourselves off to the bad, we close ourselves off to the good too.

Student A: What do you mean by armor?

Student C: It's tension, right?

Teacher: Yes, that's part of it. There is a certain amount of tension that we may construct to protect ourselves. Unfortunately, this armor can kill spontaneity if you work hard to control what happens. If you close yourself off and protect yourself physically and emotionally from people, it is difficult to let that barrier down when the opportunity to act presents itself.

Student B: Why? I've never been vulnerable and I seem to get along okay.

Teacher:	I think you have been vulnerable. At times, all humans are vulnerable. That vulnerability allows someone to react to events in his life—to grow and change.
Student B:	How can you say I've been vulnerable? You don't know me.
Teacher:	I think you have been vulnerable, because at some point you were a child.
Student B:	Yes ...
Teacher:	And would you say children are vulnerable?
Student A:	Yeah, weak and vulnerable.
Teacher:	I disagree. I believe children are very strong and resilient. They must be, otherwise they would not be able to survive the daily challenges and stresses of growing up.
Student B:	Kids don't have a lot of challenges and stresses.
Teacher:	Think about an average, active day for a child. What physical strength does he exhibit? What vocal strength? What mental and emotional strength? Just imagine the physical rigors of playing on a playground, learning to read, walk, talk, etc. Kids are incredibly strong and resilient—which means all of you are strong and resilient because you have been a child at some point in your life.
Student C:	But I thought we were talking about vulnerability.
Teacher:	Aren't children vulnerable ... emotionally, physically, spiritually?
Student C:	Yes. But I don't get how that is connected.
Teacher:	A child's whole being is connected to both strength and vulnerability from the moment he is born. Strength and vulnerability feed on one another. A child's vulnerability and openness to new things allows him to become stronger. The way in which vulnerability and openness to the influences of the world enables him to adjust, to learn, and to grow.
Student B:	Yeah, but that was a long time ago. We can't be kids again.
Teacher:	You don't need to be a child, but be *like* a child. If you feel you have lost this ability to be open to what goes on in and around you—this vulnerability—it is your job as an actor to reawaken it.
Student C:	But that seems like a very hard thing to do. It feels scary.
Teacher:	It is hard. It is scary. I never said acting was easy—it's not. But if you want to be good at it—if you want your performance to seem real, as if it is happening in that moment—then you need to allow yourself to be spontaneous and vulnerable.
Student B:	Why does your performance have to seem like it is real and happening in that moment?
Teacher:	Real life is most exciting when things do not go as planned. If your acting looks planned and predetermined and you are not responding to what is happening spontaneously in that moment, the audience will not believe

Write in your journal
using the following
prompts. Respond in detail.

- When I made eye contact
with my partner, the
emotions I felt ...
- When I made eye contact
with my partner, my
body ...
- When I touched my
partner, the emotions I
felt ...
- When I touched my
partner, my body ...
- When my partner
touched me on the
shoulder, the emotions I
felt ...
- When my partner
touched me on the
shoulder, my body ...
- When my partner
touched me on the face,
the emotions I felt ...
- When my partner
touched me on the face,
my body ...
- When my partner
touched me on the belly,
the emotions I felt ...
- When my partner
touched me on the belly,
my body ...
- When I breathed with my
partner, the emotions I
felt ...
- When I breathed with my

you. If they don't believe you, you will lose your connection with them. Their minds will wander. Good acting springs from physical, vocal, and emotional spontaneity. If you do not allow yourself to be vulnerable, it is almost impossible to be spontaneous—to react truthfully and honestly to your partner and what is happening in the scene.

Eye Contact and Touch

Acting is intimate. The word "intimate" has its origins in the Latin words *intimare* (to impress, to make familiar) and *intimus* (inmost). Intimacy is created by expressing your innermost thoughts, feelings, wants, and needs and being open to your partner's expressions of his thoughts, feelings, wants, and needs. An actor must learn to touch and be touched in order to be "familiar" with her partner. She must practice physically expressing her "innermost" thoughts, feelings, and needs. At times, the best way to express needs and wants is with physical contact.

People touch each other in real life. Drama consists of conflict and progresses in such a way that the conflict is played out. This conflict is played out through words and actions. It is very difficult to play an action without touching or being touched.

· ·

Eye Contact and Touch Exercise (This is a silent exercise.)

Step 1: Stand in actor's neutral an arm's length away from your partner, facing her.

Step 2: Look in your partner's eyes.

Step 3: Breathe in and out through your open mouth and throat.

Step 4: Do not look away from your partner. If you look away, bring your focus back to her eyes as quickly as possible. If you laugh or lose eye contact, use all of your focus and concentration to reconnect with your partner through her eyes

Step 5: Continue to make eye contact. Look deep inside your partner.

Step 6: Attempt to see the spirit in your partner's eyes. What or who do you see?

Step 7: Continue to make eye contact and put your palm on your partner's shoulder. Release a breath in and out.

Step 8: Keep your hand on your partner's shoulder and let her put a hand on your shoulder. Breathe in and out together.

Step 9: Continue to make eye contact and bring your hands to each other's cheeks. Breathe in and out together.

Step 10: Take your partner's hand and place it on your belly. Let her place your hand on her belly. Continue to make eye contact and release the breath in and out together. Release your hands.

Step 11: Hug your partner close to you and hold each other for a count of ten unison breaths. Release the embrace.

Step 12: Make eye contact again. When you feel as if your partner is ready, without speaking, break eye contact, turn away from your partner, and silently pick up your journal.

> partner, my body ...
> - When I hugged my partner, the emotions I felt ...
> - When I hugged my partner, my body ...
> - The amount of time we held each other felt like ...
> - When it was time to break the connection (eye contact) with my partner, the emotions I felt ...
> - When it was time to break the connection (eye contact) with my partner, my body ...
> - When it was time to break the connection (eye contact) with my partner, I was thinking ...
> - I liked/disliked this exercise because ...

Connecting to the Center–Impulses

Many actors, directors, and acting teachers refer to the actor's "center," or "gut." Common exclamations that are heard in a rehearsal room include things like: "Work from your center/gut," "breathe from your center/gut," "respond from your center/gut," "I'm acting from the neck up! I need to bring my head down to my center/gut." You may be told that your center/gut is in your diaphragm, or your belly, or your groin, or your buttocks. As you begin to study movement, you will be asked to explore different "centers," and you will play with letting your "center" be in your head, neck, fingers, etc.

Kristin Linklater in *Freeing the Natural Voice* spends an entire chapter on finding and releasing sound from "the Center." Close to the end of the chapter, she begins to talk about creating character:

> As you continue you will probably find that there are ex-centering aspects of feeling or character that take you away from the precise contact you have with your center, and that you become "centered" lower down or higher up in the torso ... Thus, pragmatically, it must be stated that the center is moveable." [1]

---

1   Linklater, Kristin. *Freeing the Natural Voice*. Drama Publishers, 1976.

Many beginning acting students are confused by this whole idea of "center/gut." They don't know what it is, where it is or how to access it. Let's deal first with trying to get at what the "center/gut" is and why an actor needs to care about developing a connection to it.

First, I'll throw out some words that may get your mind moving in the right direction: instinct, gut instinct, energy, energy centers, chakras, nerve endings, feelings, emotions, passion, pain, open, moving, living, breath, flow.

So, what are we getting at here? What does it mean to live, act, speak, or move from your center/gut? Let's go back to look at a child and the way she is when she is an infant. She can't talk. Her movement is limited. How and why does she communicate?

A baby or young child is wholly connected to his center. When something happens to a child, or when he has a want or need, he takes a breath and expresses his feelings. The child's natural process of expression is: **catalyst** (brain) to **impulse** (center) to **expression** (voice and whole body). As the child matures, he is told "think before you speak." The natural process of expression is short circuited, and a new process is created, which is **catalyst** (brain) to **impulse** (center) to **edit** (head) to **expression** (voice and body).

As this rerouting of the process is continually practiced, it becomes habit. A new track of expression is created. Rewards are given for the editing process—the "right" way to respond. Impulses, which possess all of the beautiful variety and color that exist in the emotional center are devalued. With years of practice for this new habit, the child reaches adulthood practiced in efficiently "skipping" the impulse step altogether. It's a lot of work to move from the head to the gut and then back up to the head. So, he may begin to take a short cut, and just stay in the head. If the impulse center is suppressed, that individual will begin to live in his head "from the neck up," and will become increasingly disconnected from the natural flow of thoughts–feelings–expressions. Without a connection to the intense emotional energy center, his expression will become progressively featureless. His voice and body will become banal and lifeless. The "fire in his belly" will be reduced to a smoldering flicker.

An actor must learn to strengthen the connection to his emotional center. He must recognize how to: reconnect the basic circuitry of **catalyst** to **impulse** to **expression**. This will enable him to diminish the editing process. With practice, he will ignite and kindle the fire in his center, which houses his: creativity, imagination, vivacity, vision, inspiration, ingenuity, originality, passion, curiosity, fascination, inventiveness, and spirit.

In order to reawaken his natural unrestricted impulses, an actor will commit to rigorous conditioning of his mind, body, and spirit. He can do this by using the work in this book and those of teachers recommended within the body of the text and in the appendix. With practice, the actor will recover his natural ability to connect to his center and respond to his impulses truthfully and spontaneously. He may then "move" his center when he plays a character who is NOT centered in the natural reservoir of human emotional life—the gut.

Basic Action—Give/Take, Push/Pull, Release/Capture/Hold

There are three basic actions that an actor employs in performance. These are the basic actions that are inherent in human relationships. The actor must train his body to fully express these actions without hesitation or intellectual analysis. Once the body is trained, it is ready to respond in an active and spontaneous manner.

The following exercises use the dynamics to explore the basic actions.

Give/Take is the action that will be addressed first, as I believe it is the most important and most difficult pair of actions to execute in a balanced manner with your scene partner(s). Most beginning actors can focus on either giving or taking in a scene, but have trouble focusing equally on both simultaneously. No one character is ever in complete control in a scene. Each character must have something at stake—he must have something to lose. If he does not have anything to lose and merely gives, gives, gives or takes, takes, takes, the scene will lack the most important element of drama: conflict. If there is no conflict, there is no drama.

NOTE: These exercises are best done on two long gymnastic mats, enabling the actors to experience full and extensive physical actions. Ample space and a supported surface allows for the physical "follow-through" that is necessary to train the actor's body for optimal expression. Using music with the exercise also makes it easier for the actor to engage his creative imagination and keep his body moving continually. Exaggeration of movement, creativity, imagination, vivacity, vision, inspiration, ingenuity, originality, passion, curiosity, fascination, inventiveness, and spirit are encouraged and are likely to enhance formidable progress and change. The connection of energy between the actors should never stop while the exercise is in progress. Imagine that every movement your partner makes is connected to you through an invisible energy force (think of strings or a river of energy connecting you together).

Floating Give/Take

Step 1: Begin in actor's neutral, making eye contact with your partner. One actor is A, the other actor is B.

Step 2: A initiates a floating movement using her entire body, sending that movement toward B (Give). B is in a ready position in actor's neutral.

Step 3: As the floating movement is sent toward him, B accepts that movement with his entire body (Take). The force of taking the movement will impact B's body to float in response.

Step 4: The taking movement then evolves into a new floating movement that B sends to A (Give) with his entire body.

Step 5: As this new floating movement is sent toward her, A accepts that movement with her entire body (Take).

Step 6: Use the entire body, not only the hands and arms or legs and feet, to float. Never lose eye contact with your partner.

Step 7: The movement never stops. Both participants float continuously in response to each other (Giving and Taking). Continue until the pair is focusing primarily on the interdependent movement of the "give and take," and secondarily on the independent movement of "give or take."

Step 8: Advanced: When the partners feel as if they are fully connected with this give–and–take action, they may move closer together and incorporate touching body parts if they so desire. Touch is not required. If you do not want to make physical contact at this point, the action can be done without it.

Pressing Push/Pull

Step 1: Begin in actor's neutral. Make eye contact with your partner. One actor is A, the other actor is B.

Step 2: B initiates a pressing movement using her entire body, sending that movement toward A (Push). A is in a ready position in actor's neutral.

Step 3: As the pressing movement is pushed toward him, A pulls that movement in with his entire body (Pull). The force of the pushing/pulling movement will impact the actor's body as they push (press toward) and pull (accept the press) in response.

Step 4: The pulling in of the press then evolves into a new pressing movement, which B sends to A (Push) with her entire body.
Step 5: As this new pressing movement is sent toward him, A pulls that movement in using his entire body (Pull).

Step 6: Avoid the urge to rely too heavily on the hands and arms to press. Maintain eye contact with your partner.

Step 7: The movement never stops. Both partners press continuously in response to each other (Push/Pull). Continue until the pair is focusing primarily on the interdependent movement of the "push and pull" and secondarily on the independent movement "push or pull."

Step 8: Advanced: When the partners feel as if they are fully connected with this push/pull action, they may move closer together and incorporate touching body parts if they so desire. Touch is not required. If you do not want to touch at this point, the action can be done without physical contact.

Flying Release/Thrusting Capture and Pressing Hold

Step 1: Begin in actor's neutral. Make eye contact with your partner. One actor is A, the other actor is B.

Step 2: B initiates a flying movement using her entire body, releasing that movement toward A (Release). A is in a ready position in actor's neutral.

Step 3: As the flying movement is released toward him, A thrusts that movement in with his entire body (Capture). A then presses the movement into his body tightly (Hold).

Step 4: The force of capturing the flying movement with a thrust and then pressing the movement into the body and holding it there will impact each actor's body.

Step 5: A then releases a flying movement to B. As the flying movement is released toward her, B thrusts that movement into herself with her entire body (Capture). B then presses the movement into her body tightly (Hold).

Step 6: Use the entire body, not just the hands and arms, to press. Maintain eye contact with your partner.

Step 7: The movement never stops. Both partners move continuously in response to each other's movements (release/capture/hold). Continue until the pair is focusing primarily on the interdependent movement of the release and capture and hold, and secondarily on the independent movement of release or captur or hold.

Step 8: Advanced: When the partners feel as if they are connecting fully with the release/capture/hold action, they may move closer together and incorporate touching body parts if they so desire. Touching is not required. If you do not want to touch at this point, the action can be done without physical contact.

Directions in Space

Our bodies move in directions in space that reflect our goals and desires, as well as our reactions to the actions and expressions of others. The direction in which an actor's body moves in her environment communicates a great deal to an audience and to her acting partners. This trajectory also generates emotional responses in the actor. These, in turn, spur visceral responses that enable her to more readily connect to her character's center. A link exists between a character's directional movement in space and the status and self-esteem of that individual. There are "high" status directions in space and "low" status directions in space.

Directions in Space Exercise

Use instrumental music with various tempos to inspire the student to explore different tempos of movement while maintaining one direction in space.

High Status Directions in Space

FORWARD

Begin in actor's neutral. On an intake of breath, begin to move your body FORWARD through the space. You may turn and twist, but the direction you move in is always FORWARD. Engage your entire body in FORWARD movement. Feel the strength, openness, and confidence of this direction. Explore the entire room moving continuously FORWARD.

Repeat for at least three to five minutes. Notice how this movement makes you feel. Compare and contrast this movement to the way you usually move through space.

HIGH

Begin in actor's neutral. On an intake of breath, begin to explore the space while you focus on moving in a HIGH direction in space. As you explore the room, imagine that your body can extend HIGHer than anything else in the room. Imagine that you tower over everything and everyone in the room. Lift yourself UP as HIGH as you can go.

Repeat for at least three to five minutes. Notice how this movement makes you feel. Compare and contrast the feeling of this movement to the way you usually move through space.

WIDE

Begin in actor's neutral. On an intake of breath, begin to move your body WIDE through space. You may turn and twist, but the direction you move in is always WIDE. Engage your entire body in WIDE movement through the space. Allow your body to make very WIDE movements, taking up as much space as possible. Feel WIDE from your toes to the top of your head.

Repeat for at least three to five minutes. Notice how this movement makes you feel. Compare and contrast the feeling of this movement to the way you usually move through space.

Low Status Directions in Space

BACKWARD

Begin in actor's neutral. On an intake of breath, begin to move your body BACKWARD through space. You may turn and twist, but the direction you move in is always BACKWARD. Engage your entire body in BACKWARD movement. Try to feel the space behind you with your back. Do not turn your head over your shoulder. The back of your body, including your head, is leading the movement.

Open response journal entry #30

Write in your journal using the following prompts. Respond in detail.

- Moving in a FORWARD direction made me feel ...
- Consistently moving in a FORWARD direction, I could imagine I was the kind of person who ...
- Moving in a FORWARD direction in space felt comfortable to me when ...
- Moving in a FORWARD direction in space felt uncomfortable to me when ...
- Moving in a FORWARD direction in space required me to ...

Open response journal entry #31

Write in your journal using the following prompts. Respond in detail.

- Use the same prompts as are listed for the forward direction, replacing FORWARD with the word HIGH.

Open response journal entry
#32

+ *Use the same prompts as are listed for the forward direction, replacing FORWARD with the word WIDE.*

Open response journal entry
#33

+ *Use the same prompts as are listed for the forward direction, replacing FORWARD with the word BACKWARD.*

Open response journal entry
#34

+ *Use the same prompts as are listed for the forward direction, replacing FORWARD with the word LOW.*

Open response journal entry
#35

+ *Use the same prompts as are listed for the forward direction, replacing FORWARD with the word NARROW.*

Repeat for at least three to five minutes. Notice how this movement makes you feel. Compare and contrast the feeling of this movement to the way you usually move through space.

LOW

Stand in actor's neutral. On an intake of breath, begin to explore the space while you focus on moving in a LOW direction in space. As you explore the room, imagine that your body can extend LOWer than anything else in the room. Imagine that you must remain beLOW everything and everyone in the room. Keep yourself DOWN as LOW as possible, while continuing to move through the space.

Repeat for at least three to five minutes. Notice how this movement makes you feel. Compare and contrast the feeling of this movement to the way you usually move through space.

NARROW

Begin in actor's neutral. On an intake of breath, begin to move your body NARROWly through the space. You may turn and twist, but the direction you move in is always NARROW. Engage your entire body in NARROW movement through the space. Compress your body to make very NARROW movements, taking up as little space as possible. Feel NARROW from your toes to the top of your head as you persist in exploring the environment.

Repeat for at least three to five minutes. Notice how this movement makes you feel. Compare and contrast the feeling of this movement to the way you usually move through space.

Stage Positions and Blocking

The location an actor occupies on the stage is referred to as his "stage position." Basic stage positions, and the shorthand used to mark them in a script, are:

Upstage: Moving away from the audience, toward the back of the stage. (U)
Downstage: Moving toward the audience, toward the front of the stage. (D)
Stage Right: Moving toward the right (facing the audience). (R)
Stage Left: Moving toward the left (facing the audience). (L)
Center stage: Moving toward the point that is in the very center of the stage (C).
Cross: Crossing the stage to a predetermined position. (X)

Thrust Stage

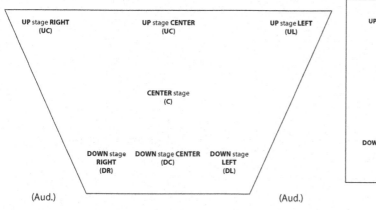

Proscenium Stage

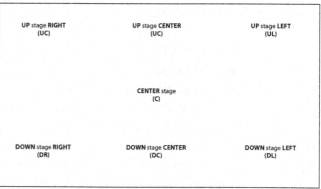

When an actor moves from one location to another on stage, that is called "blocking." Blocking created during rehearsal (either in an undirected scene or in a directed scene) that is integral to the successful completion of the scene should be written into the actor's prompt book (script) and memorized.

An example of blocking in a prompt book might look like the following (blocking is noted in **bold**.)

The following is an excerpt from *Macbeth* by William Shakespeare. (Copyright in the public domain.)

ACT I. Sc. vi

Enter Lady M—**UR**   **"Enter Lady M, UR (upstage right)"**

MACBETH   **X UR "X (cross) UR (upstage right)"**
How now! what news?

LADY MACBETH
He has almost supp'd: why have you left the chamber?

MACBETH
Hath he ask'd for me?

LADY MACBETH
Know you not he has?

MACBETH   XC "X (cross) C (center)"
We will proceed no further in this business:
He hath honour'd me of late; and I have bought
Golden opinions from all sorts of people,
Which would be worn now in their newest gloss,
 Not cast aside so soon.

LADY MACBETH
Was the hope drunk
Wherein you dress'd yourself? hath it slept since?
And wakes it now, to look so green and pale
At what it did so freely? From this time
Such I account thy love. ** Art thou afeard   ** XC "X (cross) C" (center)
To be the same in thine own act and valour
As thou art in desire? Wouldst thou have that
Which thou esteem'st the ornament of life,
And live a coward in thine own esteem,
Letting 'I dare not' wait upon 'I would,' Like the poor cat ' the adage?

MACBETH
Prithee, peace: X DL "X (cross) DL (down left)"

....

Movement Sequence with Blocking (Incorporate Music)

   1: Create a movement sequence of four to six crosses. Each cross should use a new direction
      in space.
   2: Create a movement sequence of six to eight crosses. Each cross should use a new dynamic
      and/or direction in space.

....

Living Sculpture

This exercise incorporates many aspects of acting discussed thus far in this book. The actor begins with solo work, and then she works with a partner to create a "scene."

Choose a sculpture of a person that strikes you in some way. The sculpture should be of someone's entire body. Do not choose a sculpture that is merely a bust or that shows only a portion of the subject's body. It is best to observe and walk around the original sculpture. Sculptures can be found in museums, but they may also be found in parks, government buildings, etc. Make sure that the artwork is one that you can replicate. You need to be able to put your body into the "pose" that the sculpture strikes. It is also important that you can view the sculpture in three dimensions; i.e., you should not use a picture of a sculpture, but you may use a replication or miniature of a sculpture if you must.

Living Sculpture Exercise

Session 1: (Solo)

Step 1: Observe the sculpture and memorize the position that the body is in. Look at the body from the toes to the top of the head. Write down or draw all of the specific details of how the body is placed in space, gestures, balance of weight, spine placement, etc.

Step 2: Study the sculpture. Ask yourself questions about how this body might move if it came alive. A sculpture of an individual is a snapshot of a character at one moment in time. A work of art also captures the sculptor's imagination, intent, metaphor, and meaning.

Session 2: (Solo)

Place your body in the same pose that the sculpture is in. Remain still in that position for one or two minutes.

Open response journal entry #36

Write in your journal using the following prompts. Respond in detail.

- The way in which this sculpture is placed in space makes it seem as if ...
- The gesture(s) this sculpture is creating seems to be ...
- The sculpture's weight is balanced ...
- If the sculpture came alive I imagine it would ...
- The movement before this character "froze" in the moment to create this sculpted image, I imagine the following happened ...
- If it came to life, the next movement this sculpted character would make would be ...
- This movement would lead to ...
- The five adjectives I would use to describe this person are ...
- The five adverbs I would use to describe how I imagine this character's movement are ...
- The energy this statue's pose projects into the world is ...
- This character's age /social status/ temperament is ...

Session 3: (Solo)

Begin in the sculpture's "pose." Begin to move and let your imagination take your body where it wants to go. Let your body progress through space in the way you imagine this sculpture moves. Don't set anything in stone. There are no right or wrong movements for this character. Keep in mind those things you have discovered in Sessions 1 and 2 and let them inform your movement. Allow yourself to discover new qualities of movement that are inspired by the sculpture.

Session 4: (Solo)

Begin in the sculpture's "pose." When you feel an impulse to move, let your imagination take your body where it wants to go. Repeat movements that feel as if they match your image of this sculpture's physical substance. There are still no right or wrong movements for this character, but you may find that some actions naturally assert themselves as "belonging" to this character. Keep in mind those things you have discovered in Sessions 1, 2, and 3. Let these perceptions inform your exploration. Allow yourself to discover new qualities of movement that are inspired by the sculpture.

Session 5: (Working off Another Person)

Step 1: Each actor begins in his or her statue's "pose." Explore movement together, working off each other as in the "Basic Actions" exercise. Maintain eye contact. Take in your partner's energy without allowing him to take over the scene. (Take the energy in, respond, take the energy in, respond, etc.) As you work allow your imagination to flow. Discover the who, what, when, where, how, and why of the two characters' interaction.

Step 2: Create a scene, working in this improvisational manner. Scenes have a beginning, middle, and end. Let the beginning of the scene emerge from your statue's "next" movement discussed in Session 1. Let the scene build from there as you and your partner share the space and interact with each other AS YOUR CHARACTERS.

The scene should come to a close (end) when one or both characters exits the playing area and breaks the connection.

Session 6: (Second Session with a Partner)

Use the same instructions as in Session #5. Adhere to the beginning, middle, and end points that you developed in that session. Keep your characters in the same location. What happens in between the beginning, middle, and end markers may (and probably will) change. Allow yourselves the freedom of continued exploration. Do not create a performance. Keep the work open, fluid, and improvisational.

Using Repetition Exercises

S anford Meisner was one of America's foremost acting instructors. He developed a technique for training actors while working at the Neighborhood Playhouse in New York. His technique is based on the teachings of the great Russian director and acting teacher Constantin Stanislavskyi. The Meisner technique focuses on training actors in what many call "moment–to–moment" performance. This type of realistic technique urges actors to live truthfully in the moment under imaginary circumstances. The exercises below utilize some of the beginning steps of Meisner's technique. It is the portion of the technique that is often referred to as the "repetition" exercise. This one simple exercise demands that an actor increase his ability to focus and concentrate, improve eye contact, develop trust, learn to respond truthfully and spontaneously, practice focusing on his partner, improve his ability to express impulses, and ascertain how to "take it in and let it land" before responding to his partner.

. . . .

Repetition Exercise

Part A

Step 1: Actor A sits in a chair in actor's neutral across from Actor B. They are close enough that they can see each other's eyes, but they are not touching.

Open response journal entry #39

Write in your journal using the following prompts. Respond in detail.

- What happened when my "character" began to share space with my partner's character was ...
- The "place" in which the scene takes place developed in the following way ...
- My character's main action was ...
- It felt like my partner's main action was ...
- Once we began to interact, I sensed my character's need was ...

Open response journal entry #40

Write in your journal using the following prompts. Respond in detail.

- As we continued to explore movement together, the development of the scene was influenced in the following way ...
- The relationship between the characters developed in the following ways ...

- *I was vulnerable in this scene when ...*
- *I was able to trust my partner in this scene ...*
- *Moving like this character while interacting with my partner made me feel ...*
- *The way this character interacts in this scene tells me he or she ...*

Step 2: Actor A makes a simple observation about Actor B. For example, "You have blue eyes."

Step 3: Actor B may repeat "I have blue eyes" or she may make a simple observation about Actor A. For example, "You have glasses."

Step 4: Actor A may repeat what Actor B has observed, "I have glasses," or may make a new observation about Actor B.

Step 5: This "tennis match" continues until the actors are relaxed, comfortable, not thinking, not judging, and not exerting excessive effort.

Teaching Points

a. The actor should resist the urge to pause, think, and look for something new to notice about her partner in between observations; if she does not observe something immediately, she should repeat.

b. This is not a contest. There are no winners, only collaborators.

c. Do not try to be dramatic or interesting. Keep it simple. Focus on your partner. Allow yourself to repeat and relax.

d. It is okay to say "You have blue eyes/I have blue eyes" a million times in a row. Give yourself permission to repeat and take the pressure off yourself and your partner to be "right."

e. If your partner says "You have blue eyes" and you have brown eyes, DO NOT say "I have brown eyes" or "I DO NOT have blue eyes." Simply repeat or say something about your partner.

f. You are not allowed to say anything about yourself unless your partner has just observed something about you. You can only initiate new lines that pertain to your partner.

Part B

Step 1: Repeat Steps 1–3 of Part A.

Step 2: The pair repeats this one observation until an external change occurs in either actor and it is observed by the other. For example, after repeating "You have blue eyes/I have blue eyes" a few times, Actor A smiles. Actor B notices this and says, "You smiled." Actor B repeats, "I smiled."

Step 3: The pair repeats this exchange until either actor notices another change.

Teaching Points

a. Remind yourself of points a.–f. above.

b. Allow yourself to repeat, relax, and look for changes and reactions in your partner.

c. It is okay to say, "You smiled/I smiled" a million times in a row. Give yourself permission to repeat and take the pressure off yourself and your partner to be "right" or "creative." However, I imagine that after you repeat something a few times, a change will occur. For example, the smile will change. If both actors are relaxed, open, and focused, there will be a number of external changes in just minutes.

d. You can only initiate new lines that pertain to changes you observe in your partner.

e. Limit your observations to changes that are easily observed through gesture and facial expression.

f. Let the changes happen, don't force them or consciously "make" anything happen.

- -

Part C

Step 1: Repeat steps 1–3 of Part A.

Step 2: The pair repeats this one observation until a change occurs in either actor. This change can be a noticeable external change or a change in mood. For example, "You are nervous/I am nervous," or "You are comfortable/I am comfortable."

Step 3: The pair repeats this change until either actor notices or senses another change.

- -

Teaching Points

a. Remind yourself of points a.–f. in Part A and d. in Part B.

b. This is not a contest.

c. It is okay to say "You are intrigued by me/I am intrigued by you" a million times in a row. Give yourself permission to repeat and take the pressure off yourself and your partner to be "right," but I imagine that after you repeat something a few times, a change will occur. (Something else is bound to change if you are relaxed and focused on your partner. If we are truly connecting, we change every second.)

Open response journal entry #41

Complete these journal entries after Parts A, B, and C.

Write in your journal using the following prompts. Respond in detail.

- *The most difficult part of this exercise for me is ...*
- *This is difficult for me because ...*
- *The least difficult part of this exercise for me is ...*
- *This is easy for me because ...*
- *The acting skills I practiced while doing this exercise are ...*
- *This exercise interested/ bored me because ...*
- *Watching others do this exercise, I felt ...*
- *When I was doing this exercise in front of others, I was thinking ...*
- *When I was doing this exercise in front of others, I felt ...*
- *When I was doing this exercise in front of others, my body ...*
- *The most surprising thing that happened between my partner and myself was ...*

Part 3
Acting with Text

Chapter 4
Using Memorized Lines
Without Falling into Bad Habits

Goals

Our lives are filled with goals, major and minor. Everything we do in life is done for a reason and to achieve some goal. Goals are not always obvious. Sometimes we feel as if we cruise through life on automatic pilot. We move from one day to the next without thinking about why we get up in the morning, go to work or school, talk to friends, etc. However, all of our actions have a goal or purpose. Sometimes goals do not become clear until we discover an obstacle to achieving a goal. If we are faced with a hindrance that threatens the achievement of our ambition, we struggle and search for a way to overcome this barrier.

The same is true when an actor is living on stage. Whenever he steps on stage, he must have a goal. When he is acting, his goal must be clear and crucial to him. An actor creates a condensed life. He has a limited amount of time to get what he wants. Conflict is inherent in all good drama. Therefore, the actor will face obstacles as soon as he steps on stage. There is no time to "cruise" through a play or scene, figuring out what he wants as the scene progresses. If he is not prepared, by the time he determines what his goal is, the scene (or play) will have passed. If he does not have a goal, he will not have an impact. Acting is doing. An actor must know what he wants and DO something to achieve his goal.

An actor works to find goals that he can apply to many different scenes. Later, once he learns how to analyze a scene, he will be able to align a specific goal with a specific scene.

How does he determine what goals will work for him? There are guidelines that he can follow that will help him discover the goals that work best for him. Goals should fit ALL of the criteria below. If a goal does not satisfy ALL of the criteria, it will fail.

....

Criteria for Creating Goals That Will Work

A Good Goal ...

1: Answers the question, "What do I need at this moment and from whom?"
2: Begins with the word "to."
3: Contains an action verb.
4: Can be done physically. (In other words, you need to be able to work toward achieving your goal without speaking.)
5: Is exciting or fun for you to do.
6: Must have its test in your scene partner(s). (You will know if you are getting what you want by taking in your scene partner and adjusting to his responses to what you are doing.)
7: Will not assume that your partner is in any predetermined emotional state (angry, sad, happy, etc.).
8: Has no end—it can be done forever.

....

Finding active, playable goals for a scene is a crucial acting skill to master. It take a lot of practice. Good goals are vital pieces of homework that actors bring into each rehearsal. With clear, playable goals for a scene, an actor makes herself available to "play" in rehearsals and performance.

Below is a list of ten potential goals. Five meet all of the eight criteria mentioned above (with the possible exception that you might not find it fun or exciting to do). Five do not meet all of the eight criteria.

1. I need to fall in love with my partner.
2. I need to nurture my partner.
3. I need to excite my partner.
4. I need to defeat my partner.
5. I need to kiss my partner.
6. I need to condemn my partner.
7. I need to sort of annoy my partner.
8. I need to calm my partner down.
9. I need to feel close to my partner.
10. I need to fool my partner.

Physical Actions

Once an actor has determined what goal she wants to pursue in a scene, she has some more homework to do in preparation for playing the scene. She must ask herself: "How am I going to achieve my goal?" and "What PHYSICAL ACTIONS can I do to get what I need?" It is essential that she devise a list of physical actions she can initiate to achieve her goal. These physical actions are the labor she will undertake as she works toward achieving her heart's desire—her goal. It is best for an actor to create a long list of physical actions, because her acting partner will constantly change his response to her physical actions.

Example: My GOAL is to irritate my partner. How might I do that? Some PHYSICAL ACTIONS I can attempt to irritate my partner would be: poke fun at her, crowd her, ignore her, overwhelm her, whine at her, rush at her, etc.

It is important to explore physical actions thoroughly before rehearsal with a partner. An actor cannot presume that she can achieve her goal with one physical action. Her partner will have a goal as well. It is very likely that the goals will clash. Drama is conflict. An actor will never succeed in achieving her goal if she repeatedly executes the same single physical action. If a physical action is not assisting the actor in achieving her goal, she must try something else. Physical actions affect people differently. What irritates one person may not irritate another. Also, the effect a physical action has on someone will wear off eventually, and the performer will be

- *Examine each potential goal listed. Attempt to DO each one. Determine which five meet all of the eight criteria. Write down these five goals. These are playable goals.*
- *Examine the remaining five goals. Determine which of the eight criteria the goal does not fulfill. Can it be changed in some way to make it a playable goal? Attempt to change each one and make it into an active, playable goal.*
- *Create ten active, playable goals. Confirm that each one meets ALL of the eight criteria. DO each one with a partner. Make any adjustments necessary to generate ten dynamic goals that you can use in future scene work.*

Open response journal entry #43

Write in your journal using the following prompts. Respond in detail.

- The goal that I am thinking of is ...
- I needed to achieve this goal because ...
- When I imagined myself achieving this goal, I felt ...
- When I imagined myself not achieving this goal, I felt ...
- Some of the physical actions I thought about doing to achieve this goal were ...
- Some of the physical actions I attempted to achieve this goal were ...
- The physical actions I enacted that helped me to be successful were ...
- I was aware that my physical actions were assisting me in achieving my goal because ...
- The physical actions I performed to achieve my goal that didn't assist–and might have hindered–me were ...
- I was aware that my physical actions were not helping me to achieve my goal because ...

required to try another physical action to achieve her goal. The more physical actions an actor can employ, the more successful she will be at achieving her goal. Brainstorming physical actions is the most useful way to come up with many possibilities. Brainstorming may be done alone or with others. Sometimes it is helpful to brainstorm with others, as this often produces a wide variety of options.

The key to getting what you want in life is to focus on the individual(s) who can give you what you want. The way to get what you want is to DO as many things as possible. Remember that good drama is built around conflict. Your partner's goal will create obstacles for you. You will have to work hard to get what you want. It will not be easy. This is what makes the scene exciting. Pursuing goals with physical actions will also bring your instincts and honest emotions to the surface. When obstacles arise and prevent you from getting what you need in life, your emotions become more intense. When your emotions become more intense, you are more likely to take risks. You focus on the things that you can do to get what you want.

In acting, as in life, we take cues about our success in achieving goals from our partners. An actor's awareness of verbal and nonverbal communication being sent to him by his partner is referred to as "being in the moment." The script may be predetermined. Some of your blocking may be predetermined by given circumstances. These elements are the skeleton, the bones. The skeleton, by itself, is not active. If an actor merely says his lines and does his blocking, he is not adding much life to the bones. He is lending flesh, blood, muscles, tendons, organs, etc. But something is missing. What is missing? The soul. It is an actor's job to add a living body and a soul to a performance. His goal and physical actions help to add the soul. Goals, needs, wants, desires—and the physical actions that are necessary to achieve them—are what brings the skeleton, flesh, blood, etc., to full life. They give the scene a soul. Goals, needs, wants, desires, and the physical actions that assist an actor in obtaining them are what make life exciting and worth living.

Recall a goal that you needed to achieve. It is best to choose a goal that was difficult to achieve, one which presented many obstacles and was dependent on another person. Recall the scenario in as much detail as possible. Identify the physical actions you used to achieve your goal. Complete journal entry #43.

Review the ten goals you created in journal entry #42. Choose the five that excite you most. Devise a list of AT LEAST ten physical actions that will assist you in achieving each of the five goals. Complete the following outline for each of your five chosen goals.

Testing Your Goals and Physical Actions Exercise

Step 1

a. Choose one of your goals. Review the physical actions you have imagined will work to achieve that goal.

b. Enlist a third party to assign you a partner. The partner should have a goal that conflicts with your goal. The third party should ensure that the partners do not know each other's goals.

c. Work with that partner and achieve your goal using NO WORDS.

Step 2

a. Do a. and b. from Step 1.

b. Work with that partner and achieve your goal using your body and a sound (example: ah, oo, ick, etc.). Use full vocal expression with the sound. The meaning of the sound may change, based on what happens in the scene as you interact with your partner.

Step 3

a. Do a. and b. from Step 1.

b. Work with that partner and achieve your goal using your body and a word that seems to have nothing to do with your goal (example: cabbage, singing, shoes). Use full vocal expression with the word. Use the sounds in the word to express yourself and achieve your goal. Don't get caught up in the intellectual meaning of the word. The meaning of the word may change, based on what happens in the scene as you interact with your partner.

Memorizing Lines

*I*t is very important that an actor memorize her lines exactly as they are written. An inexperienced actor may make the mistake of learning her lines incorrectly. She may think it is okay to paraphrase her lines or to "improvise" lines, as long as what she says as her line is close to what the text says or has the same intent. Do not fall into this trap. Remember that acting is a collaborative art form. Everyone is working together to communicate a message. An actor's job is to work with the text that she is given by the playwright. The playwright has worked hard to put the words together in a specific way to communicate her message. The actor's job is to lend her voice, body, and spirit to those words to bring them to life. It is not her job to rewrite the text. All of the collaborators are depending on her to perform the text as written. If she doesn't, it not only makes everyone else's job harder, it is against the law.

What? It's against the law to change the words in a play? Yes. Most scripts are copyrighted material. Actors and theater companies receive permission to perform these scripts through a contractual agreement. The contract clearly states that the script must be performed as written. If the script is not performed as written, fines can be levied or a production can be shut down.

I often throw the following question out to my classes. "If I memorize my lines incorrectly, improvise, or paraphrase, how does that make "everyone else's job harder?" These are some of the responses I have received:

"I was running lights for a show and my light cue was set to go on a line. The actor didn't say the line the way it was written, so I didn't know to change the lights."

"I was directing a drama that had a lot of sound cues of nature in it. The cues were supposed to be called when the actor said a certain word. She never said the right words at the right time, so the cues got all messed up. The audience ended up laughing at moments that were supposed to be very dramatic."

CUES

An actor in a scene or play is telling a story and/or communicating a message to the audience. His lines and movement are the part of the story that he is communicating. The actor needs to know the lines and movement by heart. He must also know where they belong in the story. If he says his line or executes his movement at the wrong time, the story will change and it may not make sense. He will also confuse his acting partners.

In many ways, creating successful drama is similar to creating an efficient machine. If a piece of a machine is missing or put into the wrong place at the wrong time, the machine will not run well and it might even break down. If you are watching a machine that is not running well or is breaking down, you don't enjoy watching it perform. Rather, you worry about what is wrong with it. The audience wants to enjoy watching a performance. They don't want to worry about what is wrong with the actors and why they look so uncomfortable, miserable, and confused. (This is how an actor often looks when someone "drops" a line or movement or says the wrong line/movement at the wrong time.)

A cue is the line or action that lets an actor know it is his turn to say his line and or initiate a particular movement. When an actor memorizes his own lines, he must also memorize his line cue and/or his action cue. If his line is evoked by words spoken by his acting partner, it is called a line cue.

Line Cues

The line cues in the example below are underlined. When these words or lines are spoken, the actor who is responding begins to respond, but her first word is not vocalized until her partner has finished his line completely.

Using the same earlier text from *Macbeth* by William Shakespeare:

ACT I. Sc. vi

MACBETH
<u>Hath he ask'd</u> for me?

LADY MACBETH
<u>Know you not</u> he has?

MACBETH
We will proceed no further in this business:
He hath honour'd me of late; and I have bought
Golden opinions from all sorts of people,
Which would be worn now in their newest gloss,
<u>Not cast aside</u> so soon.

LADY MACBETH
Was the hope drunk
Wherein you dress'd yourself? hath it slept since?
And wakes it now, to look so green and pale
At what it did so freely? From this time
Such I account thy love. Art thou afeard
To be the same in thine own act and valour
As thou art in desire? Wouldst thou have that
Which thou esteem'st the ornament of life,
And live a coward in thine own esteem,
Letting 'I dare not' wait upon 'I would,'
<u>Like the poor cat</u>' the adage?

MACBETH
Prithee, peace:

In this example, the line cue for "know you not" is "hath he asked" and so on throughout the scene. Lady Macbeth should begin her line as Macbeth says the last word of his line, "me." Her response and the physical intake of breath begins on the line cue, but her line is not uttered until Macbeth has completed his line. If she comes in too early with her line, it is called "jumping on your partner's line." Cutting your partner off before he finishes his lines is disrespectful and shows a lack of consideration for him. Keep the energy going. Build the intensity of the scene by reacting before, while, and after you speak. But let the words wait their turn. You have plenty of other tools to use. ALL of the words have been included in the script by the playwright for a good reason. A good actor values the script and his fellow collaborators enough to respect ALL of the words and their place in the script. Learning your lines and cues in this manner will keep the energy flowing in the scene when it is performed or rehearsed, it will eliminate unnecessary pauses between lines (which may lead to a void on stage or overacting), and reflects realistic human interaction.

A word about pauses: It is okay, and often necessary, to pause before you say a line or between lines. All pauses must be filled with the energy of actively pursuing a goal. The pause must exist for a good reason and should push the audience to the edges of their seats, wondering "what is going to happen next?" They will expect something significant to follow a pause. If what occurs after a pause doesn't "top" the pause, the audience's energy will drop, they will feel let down, and you will have to work hard to "win" them back.

A word about rushing your lines: An inexperienced actor may rush through her lines and take no pauses. This may frustrate her audience because it sounds as if all of the lines are the same. The audience may feel overwhelmed. They need time to absorb language and action. They need some pauses.

Physical Cues

If your line is evoked by something that someone does—a physical action or event that takes place—it is called a physical cue.

Example: The physical cue is underlined. When this action occurs, the actor who is responding begins to respond immediately.

ACT I. Sc. vi

Macbeth sees Lady Macbeth [1]

MACBETH
How now! what news?
LADY MACBETH
He has almost supp'd: why have you left the chamber?

Action Cue

An actor's action cue is the word or words that act as a catalyst for the actor to speak. These cues move the actor to say his next line as part of the physical action he is using to achieve his goal.

Learning cues by rote is as necessary as learning lines by rote. As an actor practices his script, he should use his line, physical, and action cues to prompt him.

---

1   Shakespeare does not include stage directions that are separate from the text. We know that Macbeth sees Lady Macbeth because he asks her a question that implies this action.

WAYS TO MEMORIZE LINES

Recording: Many professional actors record their lines and then listen to them whenever possible. I have had much success memorizing lines by listening to recorded lines on headphones/earbuds as I do something physical (working out, folding laundry, playing a sport, etc.). I also suggest that actors listen to lines as they sleep. This requires little effort and the lines tend to become securely lodged in the actor's subconscious mind, which is where you want them to be.

Writing: I always tell actors that the more senses they involve in the memorization process, the better. Writing your lines down in your own handwriting uses your sense of touch to connect with your lines.

Speaking and moving with a friend or acting partner: Ask a friend to be "on book" and run your lines with you as much as possible. Ask them to read the line, action, or physical cue that prompts your line. When you are doing this, don't sit down—allow yourself to move about.

CAUTION: DO NOT close your eyes when you memorize your lines. Some people learn to memorize in this way. They will look at something, and then close their eyes and try to remember it. Often when an actor memorizes in this way, he is memorizing his lines on a very conscious and superficial level. When he gets into a scene and has to multitask (pursue his goal with his physical actions, do his blocking, be aware of his "as if," etc.), he forgets his lines and gets very flustered. Keep your eyes open and incorporate as many senses as possible when you are memorizing (speak, move, hear, see, etc.).

What? It's against the law to change the words in a play? Yes. Most scripts are copyrighted material. Actors and theater companies receive permission to perform these scripts through a contractual agreement. The contract clearly states that the script must be performed as written. If the script is not performed as written, fines can be levied or a production can be shut down.

Working with Open Scenes

What is an open scene? An open scene is a scene that has no meaning. In an open scene, there are no given circumstances. The lines in an open scene do not give the actors any clues as to who the characters are, what is happening at the moment, what has happened the moment before the scene begins, what will happen after the scene ends, where the scene is set, etc. The lines in an open scene must be memorized by rote, with no intention or inflection. An open scene is like the bones of a skeleton. In order for a bunch of bones to take shape and have meaning, they need to be assembled in a certain order. Memorizing the open scene is the process of putting the skeleton together in a particular order. Once the skeleton of the scene is assembled (memorized by rote) and given voice by living, breathing people (the actors), a real moment (scene) can be achieved by adding emotion and spirit (goals, physical actions, as if). A strong foundation—lines memorized by rote—are the bones upon which the living scene must be built.

Memorize the following open scene (Parts A and B) by rote, with no inflection and no meaning. No question marks, exclamation points, etc. have been included in the text, and they should not be added by the actor when he memorizes the scene. He will know he has memorized the scene by rote if he can say the lines: while doing some physical activity (playing a sport, folding clothes, shuffling and dealing cards, etc.), while walking backwards, when speaking at a rapid speed, without pausing between the lines, etc. In other words, he is done memorizing when he is able to say the lines in order while his mind and body is focused on another task.

Open Scene #1

A: I can feel it in the air.
B: What.
A: You know.
B: Hmm.
A: That's what you told me.
B: When.
A: Before.
B: Hmm.
A: You know you did. Stop it.
B: I'm not doing anything.
A: No.
B: No.
A: I need to leave.
B: Leave.
A: I will.
B: It seems like a good idea.
A: Well, it isn't right.
B: I'm sorry.
A: Right.
B: So long.
A: See you later, I guess.

Open response journal entry #46

Write in your journal using the following prompts. Respond in detail.

- *When I try to achieve my goal with only movement ...*
- *When I try to achieve my goal with movement and sound ...*
- *When I try to achieve my goal with movement and one word ...*
- *When I try to achieve my goal with movement and the text from the open scene ...*

Using the Open Scene to Test Your Goals and Physical Actions

Step 1: Use the "Testing your goals and physical actions exercise" Steps 1, 2, and 3.

Step 2: Use the lines in Open scene #1 with your partner. One actor should be Part A and one should be Part B. Remember, the words have no meaning until you *give* them meaning. When you have a goal and physical actions and a partner to work off of, the words will take on meaning as they become an additional tool (along with your voice and movement) that will assist you in achieving your goal and responding to your partner.

Personalization–"As If"–Justification

An actor pursuing his goal by using physical actions, meeting up with obstacles, and attempting to overcome these obstacles in order to achieve his goal keeps a performance alive and interesting. He may find that he knows what he wants and has thought about how to get it, but he is getting stuck. He is convinced that the physical action he has chosen will work. He continues to use this one physical action over and over again in an attempt to achieve his goal in the scene. He may enact this physical action with more intensity (louder, faster, more aggressively, etc.), believing that eventually it will work. He begins to feel like he is beating his head against a brick wall, expecting to create a hole in the wall. I have never seen a head make a hole in a brick wall, no matter how hard, fast, or often they come into contact. By this point, the actor is usually so stuck and frustrated that he cannot recall any of the additional physical actions on the list that he prepared for homework.

It is time for this actor to engage his imagination. There is nothing that will help him more than his imagination. His imagination is connected to his center and it wakes his unconscious and unlimited passion. The actor needs to use his imagination to create an "as if" that will match his goal and physical actions. A good specific "as if" will personalize the scene and persuade his subconscious mind that there is a very good reason (justification) for him to pursue his chosen goal. A very specific "as if" can light a scene on fire because it brings personal needs into play.

Example: Let's continue with the scene from Macbeth.

I am playing Lady Macbeth, a woman who will do anything to obtain power. I am preparing for the scene where I am convincing my husband to murder someone so that my husband and I can sit on the throne of Scotland.

My goal: to bend my husband to my will.

My physical actions: humiliate, harass, seduce, bribe, overpower, shame, torment, bully, worry, pester, provoke.

As an individual, I don't care about obtaining power and I can't think of a time when I would try to convince someone I love to kill a friend in order to acquire power. I may not be particularly interested in bending my significant other to my will. But, can I imagine a situation in which I might want to do this? Yes. I will create an "as if" from either my own personal experience or from my imagination.

My "as if": It's as if I am a severe diabetic and I have become pregnant. The doctor has told my significant other and me that I might die if I carry this baby. I have always wanted to be a mother and I know in my heart that I could not live with myself if I terminated the pregnancy. My significant other has never wanted to be a parent and does not want to lose me. I must "bend" my significant other to my will in order to keep both my significant other and the baby.

This "as if," and the powerful emotions it evokes, will fuel all that I do to achieve my goal in the scene. My goal, physical actions, and "as if" will give life, meaning, and texture to the scene. I have created an imaginary situation that makes the goal and desire of Lady Macbeth very credible, urgent, and vital to me personally. I have a justification for my goal and physical actions. I have a very personal reason WHY I want what I want.

Memorize Open Scene #2.

Open Scene #2

A: Did you hear that.

B: What.

A: That, that.

B: I can't hear anything.

A: You are being serious.

B: Think.

A: I don't know.

B: Think.

A: I said, I don't know.

B: I know what you said.

A: Then why.

B: Are you being serious.

A: Don't say that.

B: Don't say what.

A: That, that.

B: I need to stop this.

A: Okay, go.

B: Really.

A: Yes.

Open response journal entry #47

Write in your journal using the following prompts. Respond in detail.

- My goal for this scene is ...
- My physical actions are ...
- My "as if" is ...
- Adding an "as if" when performing the scene allowed me to ...

"As If" Exercise

Step 1: Review Steps 1 and 2 for "Using the Open Scene to Test Your Goals and Physical Actions."

Step 2: Create an "as if" to justify and personalize your goal and physical actions in the scene.

Step 3: Perform the scene with a partner.

Gestures

"Now that I am saying words, my body is frozen. What do I do with my hands?"

As a new actor begins to work with words, sometimes her body freezes and she attempts to achieve her goal using only the words of the text, her head, and facial expression. This leads to a great deal of tension and very unnatural behavior. This type of performance is often called "acting from the neck up."

A beginning actor may sense this tension and start to think about how stiff and immobile her body has become. She may begin to wonder, "What do I do with my hands?"; "Should I sit?"; "Should I stand?"; "Should I move around a lot?"; "Should I make big expressions with my hands and face so that the audience can see me?" These thoughts only make matters worse, keeping her focused on the wrong person—herself—and locking her into the fears that exist in her mind.

When questions like this begin to pop up, it is time to get back to the basics of relaxation and movement. First, it is imperative that she warm up her body to free herself of excess tension. She must also reacquaint her body with the freedom to express the many gestures that are a part of life, gestures that may be unfamiliar to her.

The four types of gesture are:

1. **SOCIAL GESTURES** are the types of gestures used at social gatherings, such as funerals, weddings, football games, coronations, or everyday activities. Some examples include: a hand-shake, a hug, a kiss, a bow, worshipping, etc.

2. **FUNCTIONAL GESTURES** are activities such as dressing, putting on makeup, washing clothes, shaving, etc. Many professions use specific gestures, such as a waitperson, a bartender, a chimney sweep, a construction worker, a writer, etc.

3. **EMOTIONAL GESTURES** put the body in a position that represents a particular emotion. The actor should not "try to feel" the emotion, but should create a movement that expresses a particular emotion. Emotions such as grief, joy, hatred, fear, etc., arouse strong visual images of what the physicality of that emotion might be. It is sometimes helpful for actors to include candid still photographs of people responding to major life events. These photographs reveal how the body expresses powerful emotion.

4. **MOTIVATIONAL GESTURES** physically express a desire or need, "physicalized" in an archetypal pose. Examples include: to get love, to gain acceptance, to dominate, to take revenge, etc.

The following is an exercise that helps to free an actor physically, and will help her to reconnect with the freedom of ever expansive physical expression.

....

Full-Body Gesture Exercise

Step 1: Begin with a list of five or six examples of each of the four types of gestures. If you are working on a specific role, you may look for gestures which are noted in the script's stage directions, or you may create a list of gestures that might be used by the character you are playing.

Step 2: Choose musical accompaniment that will inspire impassioned physical expression. This will help the actor to get out of her head and into her body.
a. Take one gesture from the list created.
b. Use your whole body to create that gesture.
c. Begin with a "normal"-sized expression of that gesture.
d. Repeat going in and out of the gesture.
e. As you repeat the gesture, begin to make it larger and more extreme.
f. Continue to move in and out of the gesture.
g. Find specific physical movements that manifest that gesture and continue to repeat those movements fluidly and automatically. Fine tune the gesture down to just three very specific movements.
h. Allow your body to become familiar with and memorize this overexaggerated manifestation of the gesture.

Step 3:
a. Add a vocalized sound to the gesture. Repeat the sound and the gesture, making them one.
b. Repeat the sound and gesture using variations. For example: fast movement and full voice, fast movement and soft voice, large movement and sharp voice, etc.
c. Bring the gesture back to what you imagine "normal" size would be. Connect the gesture to a word.
d. Repeat the word and the gesture, using the whole body. Be aware of the freedom. Stay in your body, avoid moving into your head because you are incorporating a word.

Step 4:
a. Repeat with a different type of gesture, new sound, and new word from your list.
b. Explore at least one of each of the four types of gestures this way.
c. Repeat this exercise often, using various gestures.

....

Nerves

The first time an actor presents a scene in front of an audience, she is bound to be nervous. Everyone is nervous to some extent. Nerves are good, they give the actor energy (see the "Fear and Exhilaration" section.) However, she does not want her nerves to get in the way of her performance. She wants the energy from the nerves to fuel the performance. She cannot make nerves go away by telling them to. The more the actor focuses on her nerves or tries to ignore them, the more powerful they become.

There are some things our actor can do to help lessen the nerves she feels:

1. Ensure that she has prepared to the best of her ability.
2. Review her rehearsal charts and make sure she has done all of her homework.
3. Come prepared and so well rehearsed that she does not need to think about her lines, her goals, her physical actions, her "as if," etc.
4. Now it is time to PLAY. Thinking of her performance as "playing"—which it is, of course—brings her focus to where it should be.
5. In the scene, the actor's focus should be on her partner, reacting to her partner, getting what she wants from her partner, and enjoying the thrill of human interaction. If her focus and concentration is on all of these things, she will not have time to be nervous when she is performing.
6. Whatever she does, she SHOULD NOT focus on herself and how she looks, or sounds, or anything that the audience might "see" about her. That is out of her control at this point. IF she has trained her body and voice, IF she has done her homework and rehearsed, IF she has done a physical and vocal warm-up before she begins, THEN she will be fine and she will probably enjoy and be exhilarated by performing. If not, she has just discovered that acting is not for her. That is okay. She can still benefit from all that she has learned. Actor training can aid her in many areas of her life.

Staying *In The Moment*

What to Do if You (or Your Scene Partner) Mess Up

Embrace the mistakes. Keep going. Focus on your partner. Don't stop. Sometimes making a mistake—dropping a line, not having the right prop, being in the wrong place—can add life to a scene that has become too automatic. Mistakes can actually "breathe new life" into a scene. Often, when mistakes are made, an actor's focus becomes more intense. She has to think on her feet. This is good. This type of heightened alertness can add an element of additional energy to the performance. Life is filled with mistakes. The way a person moves on with living and reacts to those unexpected blunders is what makes human existence dynamic. So, press on! If you are prepared and have created a firm foundation, then you and your partner will find your way. And the good news is that the journey is often exhilarating.

> *Open response journal entry #48*
>
> *Write in your journal using the following prompts. Respond in detail.*
>
> - *I explored the (choose one: social, functional, emotional, motivational) gesture ...*
> - *When I began, my body ...*
> - *When I began, I felt ...*
> - *I felt fully connected to my body and lost inhibitions when ...*
> - *When I incorporated sound, my gesture ...*
> - *When I incorporated a word from the text, my gesture ...*
> - *The parts of my body that felt the most free and expressive were ...*
> - *When I finished, my body ...*
> - *When I finished, I felt ...*

Chapter 5

How to Approach Scene Work

Acting Etiquette—Respect, Hard Work, and Discipline

Undirected Scene Work

A beginning actor is quickly required to work on a scripted scene with her classmates, without a director. This is called undirected scene work. When she is asked to do undirected scene work, she should think of it as a tool she is using to hone her skills as an actor. It isn't necessary to create a polished performance that will impress her peers. It is important for her to give her best effort and apply the tools she has learned. Undirected scenes, like open scenes, are tools an actor uses to practice her process. Striving for the "product" of an audience-ready performance will only pull her focus away from where it should be—on her "process."

Here are some suggestions for getting the most out of working on an undirected scene:

1. Show up ON TIME for all rehearsals and come prepared to work.
2. DO YOUR HOMEWORK:
    a. Memorize your lines by rote.
    b. Decide what your character wants in the scene (goal).
    c. Decide what you can physically do with each line to get what you want (physical actions).
    d. Create an "as if" in order to personalize your goal and connect yourself more deeply to your need to obtain your goal.
    e. Know exactly what your relationship is to your partner. Make the relationship very specific. For example: Kent is my younger brother, whom I have never felt close to because he favors my mother over my father.
    f. Know the setting of your scene. Again, be very specific. For example: I am in the house of my very rich boyfriend and it is filled with very expensive furniture that I can't afford to replace.
    g. Know what has happened the moment before the scene begins. What is the catalyst for the scene?
    h. Determine what props and set/costume pieces are absolutely necessary for the scene and rehearse with them.
    i. Endow the props, costumes, and set pieces you will use in your scene.
3. Focus on your partner at all times while you are playing the scene. This will help you to relax and remove unnecessary pressure to "perform."
4. Be open to your scene partner in rehearsal: make eye contact, touch, focus, concentrate, trust your partner, allow yourself to be vulnerable, take risks.
5. Respond truthfully and spontaneously to what your partner is DOING and saying.
6. NEVER reveal your goal, physical actions, or "as if," to your partner. If they try to guess, do not confirm that they are right or wrong. Don't kill all of the excitement and conflict in the scene.
7. Run lines with your partner in neutral. Don't give yourself or your partner a line reading (how to say a line).
8. Listen to your partner.
9. Watch your partner.
10. Take your partner in and let what he is doing land, THEN respond.

11. Trust your impulses. Trust your "gut," and don't think too much when you are working on the scene. Do your thinking when you are doing your homework, not when you are living in the scene with your partner.

12. Let go of the "shoulds" to yourself:

> "I should look like this on this line."
>
> "I should sit here."
>
> "I should stand here."
>
> "I should be sad."

Let go of the "shoulds" to your partner:

> "You should move over here."
>
> "You should touch me on this line."
>
> "You should be meaner to me," etc.

13. Never blame anyone—and whatever you do, don't ever blame your partner. If the scene isn't working, look at what you need to do to make it work.

- Try a different goal, physical actions, or "as if."
- Make more eye contact.
- Touch more.
- Focus more.
- Concentrate more.
- Be more vulnerable.
- Take more risks and trust your partner more.

14. NEVER tell your partner what to do. He has a mind and imagination of his own. Variety is the spice of life. If all of the ideas for the scene come from one person, the acting will not ring true and will be less exciting than if each player contributes.

15. If everyone in the scene has done his homework and is really trying, something will happen.

16. Remember, you are practicing your skills. No matter what happens in a scene, you can always practice some aspect of acting. Work with what you have right in front of you.

Given Circumstances

Given circumstances are the *who, what, when, where,* and *how* of a scene. They are the details that are written into the script by the playwright or given to the performer by the director/designer in a production. These details communicate to the reader/player *what* is happening, *where* it is happening, to *whom* it is happening, *when* it is happening, *how* it is happening, etc. These details also include any of the specifics that are available in the text about a character's history, the setting's history, etc. The given circumstances are "given" to the actor. They should not be altered or changed.

Imaginary Circumstances/Filling in the Blanks

The playwright gives the actor some given circumstances, but what the writer gives him is not an entire life. It is vital that an actor use his imagination to flesh out the character and make him or her a real live human being. Once you have reviewed and studied the information in the text, use your imagination to flesh out your character. For example, if your character is poor and has always been poor, how do you think that affects him? Or if your character is poor and was once rich, how does that influence who she is? Actors must be curious. Create your character's world, life, and history with painstaking detail. Imagine you are a detective and you need to create all of the details that lead up to the events in the scene. If you create passionate and exciting images, your acting will also be passionate and exciting.

At times, a playwright will write only part of a line in a script.

EXAMPLE: *The Importance of Being Earnest* by Oscar Wilde (copyright in the public domain)
Act 1

JACK
And I would like to be allowed to take advantage of Lady Bracknell's temporary absence …

GWENDOLEN
I would certainly advise you to do so. Mamma has a way of coming back suddenly into a room that I have often had to speak to her about.

JACK
[Nervously.] Miss Fairfax, ever since I met you I have admired you more than any girl … I have ever met since … I met you.

The actor must "fill in the blanks" of these lines. He must decide what the character would say if he had continued. He should write the section of the line that is written as "…" (an ellipsis) and memorize this "fill-in." If the ellipsis is written at the end of a line, this is often an indication that the other actor interrupts him mid-sentence. If this is the case, he may be required to continue his line if his partner forgets to cut him off. He will certainly need to continue the thought and energy of the incomplete line. Having thought about and actually recorded what words would replace the ellipsis helps the actor to continue the thought and energy of the dialogue.
Have fun!

The Moment Before

In life, when you enter a room or meet someone, you know exactly where you have been and what has happened to you the moment before. The moment before is usually the most clear and palpable thing on your mind when you move into the next moment, the next task at hand. Whatever has just happened to you, wherever you have just been, will influence how you react to where you are. Life is a series of moments that are linked together. No matter how much we plan for each day or even each moment in our lives, we cannot control life. This is because we live life with other people, animals, technology, nature, etc. All living elements in life are volatile and constantly changing. To make a character alive and in this moment, an actor must know what the character has experienced in the moment before. His response in the moment will be influenced by what has happened to him, where he has been, whom he has encountered, etc. As an actor is entering a scene, he should not only know what he wants, but what has happened the moment before he is seen by the audience and the other characters on stage. The more interesting he makes the moment before, the more interesting his entrance will be. An actor should not share his moment before with his acting partner(s).

EXAMPLE: Your character is about to get married. The moment before he enters the room where the ceremony takes place, his best friend tells him that his future spouse was convicted as a teen of brutally murdering an elderly couple while they were asleep in their home.

Raising the Stakes, Increasing Intensity, and Making Exciting Choices

*I*f an actor feels as if his scene is dragging, boring, or his actions are not exciting to play, he would do well to review his "as if." His "as if" needs to stimulate him to action NOW. When he imagines his "as if," it should make his blood boil. Sometimes an actor will choose an "as if" that does not mean much to him personally, or is not compelling to him. This does not mean the "as if" will not work. Sometimes all that is needed in a scene to make it more playable and interesting is increasing the intensity or "raising the stakes" for the character. This is usually best done by using the imagination to create an "if/then" that will electrify the situation.

How to Raise the Stakes and Increase the Intensity in a Listless Scene

- Review your goal.
- Is the language you are using specific and exciting to you?
- Do you feel enthusiastic and aroused to action by your goal? Your physical actions? Your "as if?" If not, change these aspects of your scene until you are adrenalized just thinking about your choices.
- If a choice you have made has become dull and listless, CHANGE IT. There are countless options for playing each and every scene ever created.
- Are you copying someone else's work or using someone else's ideas (such as your partner)? DON'T. You are an individual and you cannot force yourself to be hooked on someone else's choices.

Being Specific

Endowing, Sense Memory, and Substitution—Using Costume, Set, and Prop Pieces

If an actor is going to use costume, set, or prop pieces in her scene, it is important that she endow them with some significant meaning. This is part of the "specific" work that will give her scene texture and will transform something that is imaginary into something real to the actor, and subsequently to the audience. A large component of good acting is accepting make-believe. This is why children can create such realistic performances. If a young boy wants to play Superman, he puts a piece of material on his back and believes the material is a cape that gives him the ability to fly when he plays the role of this superhero. In his mind, he has endowed the piece of material with super powers. Believing his "cape" has been invested with super powers helps him believe he is Superman.

It is the same with an actor of any age. He must believe in the make-believe of the set, costumes, and prop pieces that are used in a performance. An actor's costumes must be regarded as the clothing that his character has chosen to wear. He must know what that clothing means to him. He may ask himself, "Where did it come from?"; "Did someone I love give me this?"; "Do I want to use/wear this, or am I required to by some outside force (parent, boss, teacher, etc.)?"; "What memories does this item stir up?" The more significant each element is in the character's life, the easier it will be for the actor to believe in the make-believe world he has created.

Stage Directions

When you begin to work on published scripted text, you will most likely find that stage directions are written into the text in italics and/or parenthesis.

Example: *Waiting for Godot* by Samuel Beckett[1]

ACT I. Sc. i

A country road. A tree.

Evening.

Estragon, sitting on a low mound, is trying to take off his boot. He pulls at it with both hands, panting.

He gives up, exhausted, rests, tries again.

As before.

Enter Vladimir.

---

1   Beckett, Samuel. *Waiting For Godot*. Grove Press. NY. 1954. pp. 1–2.

ESTRAGON:

(*giving up again*). Nothing to be done.

VLADIMIR:

(*advancing with short, stiff strides, legs wide apart*). I'm beginning to come round to that opinion. All my life I've tried to put it from me, saying Vladimir, be reasonable, you haven't yet tried everything. And I resumed the struggle. (*He broods, musing on the struggle. Turning to Estragon.*) So there you are again.

ESTRAGON:

Am I?

VLADIMIR:

I'm glad to see you back. I thought you were gone forever.

ESTRAGON:

Me too.

VLADIMIR:

Together again at last! We'll have to celebrate this. But how? (*He reflects.*) Get up till I embrace you.

Sometimes a playwright will incorporate very specific stage directions into his script and he will expect that the actor follow those stage directions exactly. The example given above demonstrates this. Samuel Beckett was incredibly specific about his stage directions, and he threatened to close down productions that did not follow the stage directions he wrote into his plays. These stage directions can supply an actor with important information that helps to fulfill the playwright's intention. In plays that do not rely primarily on text to communicate a message, stage directions are crucial to maintaining the playwright's message, metaphor, and meaning.

A NOTE ON STAGE DIRECTIONS

Sometimes published contemporary scripts include stage directions that are added to a script during the original production of the play. When working on a production, the actor should follow the advice of his director as he decides whether or not to follow all of the stage directions that are written into the script.

If a student is working on a scene to practice technique, the stage directions can sometimes limit the actor's training process. If this is the case, it is advisable for acting students to cross out stage directions that require specific blocking, movements, or emotional responses. Beginning actors will rely too heavily on these directions and will not exercise the tools that have been suggested in this book to train their instruments and awaken their creative spirits.

Rehearsing

The following charts are meant to be completed after every rehearsal to aid in the beginning actor's process. Most scenes will be rehearsed more than 2 or 3 times. Copies of the charts may be made for additional rehearsals.

High Score Success

	REH #	REH #	
1. I showed up on time for reharsal and was prepared to work	_____	_____	
2. I ran through my lines in neutral with my partner before we began to work the scene	_____	_____	
3. I kenw my lines by role	_____	_____	
4. The goal used in this reharsal is a good goal to use in this scene	_____	_____	1 = strongly agree
5. I used a new physical actiions for each line to achieve my goal			2 = agree
The physical actions I used helped me to achieve my goal	_____	_____	3 = disagree
6. I have more physical actions in mind that I can use next time we rehearse	_____	_____	4 = strongly disagree
7. I fell that, at times, I was working to achieve my goal	_____	_____	5 = didn't do this
8. I was excited and interested when I was working to achieve my goal	_____	_____	
9. I know what my character's relatioinship is to the other character. I have made this relationship very specific	_____	_____	
10. The setting we have chosen makes the scene both exciting and beliveable to me	_____	_____	
11. I have endowed the setting	_____	_____	
12. The props I'm using in the scene are necessary and help me	_____	_____	
13. I have endowed my props	_____	_____	
14. The costume pieces I'm using in the scene are necessary and help me	_____	_____	
15. I have endowed my costume pieces	_____	_____	
16. My 'as if' makes it easier for me to pursue my goal and makes the scene feel more true to me	_____	_____	

Low Score Success

	Rehearsal #	Rehearsal #	Rehearsal #	
1. I felt that I achieved my goal early in the scene and had nothing to do for the remainder of the scene	_____	_____	_____	Make copies of this chart and include a self- evaluation for each time you rehearse with your scene partner(s)
2. I was bored rehearsing the scene	_____	_____	_____	
3. I told my partner what my goal is	_____	_____	_____	
4. I told my partner what my physical actions are	_____	_____	_____	1 = strongly agree
5. I told my partner what my "as if" is	_____	_____	_____	2 = agree
6. I had a hard time remembering what my goal and felt as if I was trying to create my "as if"	_____	_____	_____	3 = disagree
7. Once I started playing the scene, I couldn't remember what my "as if" was	_____	_____	_____	4 = strongly disagree 5 = didn't do this
8. I told my partner what to do in the scnene	_____	_____	_____	Review your scores on the chart. If you have rated an item
9. I helped my partner figure out how to say some of their lines in the scene	_____	_____	_____	3 or above, keep doing what you are doing with these
10. I let my partner tell me what to do	_____	_____	_____	aspects of your work.
11. I let my partner tell me how to say some of my lines	_____	_____	_____	Items you have rated lower than
12. The scene is not working and it is my fault	_____	_____	_____	3 are items you need to focus on more intently as you continue
13. The scene is not working, and it is my partner's fault	_____	_____	_____	to work.
14. The scene is working because of what I am doing	_____	_____	_____	Please review earlier chapters to discover what you need to
15.. The scene is working because of what my partner is doing	_____	_____	_____	change about your work.

When and How to Start and Stop

When presenting a scene, it is best to "just do it." Giving a long introduction or explanation of what has happened before the scene begins is unnecessary. An actor's job is to let the audience experience him acting, not explaining. Too much explanation will bring the actor—and his audience—into their heads.

Here are a few suggestions on when and how to start and stop your scene.

BEFORE SHOWING THE SCENE TO AN AUDIENCE

- Make all of your decisions BEFORE the day of your presentation.
- Discuss any aspects of set-up or flow of the scene in rehearsal.
- When you rehearse the scene, include all of the details: props, set pieces, costume pieces, location of entrances and exits, required blocking, how you will start and stop the scene, etc. (This is called a "dress rehearsal.")

THE DAY YOU SHOW YOUR SCENE TO AN AUDIENCE

- Set up your stage ahead of time, if possible.
- Get dressed in any required costume pieces in advance, if possible.
- Make sure you preset all of your props for the scene so they are where you want them to be when you need them.
- Ask if there is a space to do a short physical and vocal warm-up BEFORE it is time for you to present your scene.
- When it is your turn to present, take your place for the beginning of the scene (on stage or off stage), remind yourself of "the moment before," and wait for the audience to be quiet.
- Once the audience is quiet, begin the scene, bringing the energy of "the moment before" into that first moment of the scene.
- Remember: The beginning is always the initiation of the physical actions the actors will use to achieve their goals, not necessarily the first line.
- Work your way through the scene—do not stop until you get to the end.
- When you get to the end of the scene, pause for a moment and be still.
- Take a breath.
- Join your partner, face the audience, and bow.
- Exit the playing area.

Congratulations! You have just completed the first steps of the long and enjoyable journey of experiencing the art of acting as a NATURAL ACTOR.

Appendix

Resources for further reading and exploration

Artist's Journaling Practice

Cameron, Julia. *The Artist's Way*. G.P. Putnam's Sons, New York. 1992

Voice

Linklater, Kristin. *Freeing the Natural Voice: Imagery and Art in the Practice of Voice and Language*. Drama Pub; Revised and Expanded edition October 2006.

Berry, Cecily. *Voice and the Actor*. MacMillan Publishing, New York. 1973.

Berry, Cecily. *The Actor and his Text*. Harrap, Ltd., London. 1988

Lessac, Arthur. *The Use and Training of the Human Voice*. Drama Book Publishers, New York. 1960.

Rodenburg, Patsy. *The Right to Speak*. Methuen Drama, London. 1992

Eisenson, Jon. *Voice and Diction*. MacMillan Publishing. 1985

Movement and Body Work

Suzuki, Tadashi. *The Way of Acting*. Theatre Communications Group. 1986

Gelb, Michael. *Body Learning*. Henry Holt & Co., New York. 1981

Chekhov, Michael. *To the Actor, on the Technique of Acting*. Routledge, 2002.

Spolin, Viola. *Improvisation for the Theatre, 3rd edition*. Northwestern University Press. 1999

Advanced Acting Techniques

Stanislavski, Konstantin. *An Actor's Work*. Translated and edited by Jean Benedetti. Routledge. London & New York. 2010.

Stanislavski, Konstantin. *An Actor Prepares, Creating a Role, Building a Character*. Translated by Elizabeth Reynolds Hapgood. Theatre Arts Books (Routledge), New York. 1964.

Meisner, Sanford. *On Acting*. Vintage Books. New York. 1987.

Hagen, Uta. *Respect for Acting , 2nd edition* Wiley Publications. 2008.

Hagen, Uta. *A Challenge For The Actor*. Charles Scribner's Sons; 10th Impression edition 1991.

Adler, Stella. *The Technique of Acting*. Bantam, 1990.

Adler, Stella. *The Art of Acting*. Applause Books, 2000.

Boleslavsky, Richard. *Acting; The first six lessons*. Theatre Arts Books, New York. 1933.

Carnovsky, Morris. *The Actor's Eye*. Performing Arts Journal Publications, New York. 1984.

Bruder, Melissa, et al. *A Practical Handbook for the Actor*. Vintage Books. 1986.

Shakespeare

Barton, John. *Playing Shakespeare*. Methuen Publishing, London. 1984.

Linklater, Kristin. *Freeing Shakespeare's Voice*. Theatre Communications Group. 1992.

CPSIA information can be obtained
at www.ICGtesting.com
Printed in the USA
BVOW04s1823110917

494567BV00003B/74/P